How to Make a Parai

CRITICAL AUTHORS & ISSUES

Josué Harari, Series Editor

A complete list of books in the series
is available from the publisher.

How to Make a Paranoid Laugh

Or, What Is Psychoanalysis?

François Roustang

Translated by Anne C. Vila

PENN

University of Pennsylvania Press

Philadelphia

Publication of this volume was assisted by a grant from the
French Ministry of Culture.

Originally published 1996 as *Comment faire rire un paranoïaque?*
Copyright © 1996 Éditions Odile Jacob

10 9 8 7 6 5 4 3 2 1

Published by
University of Pennsylvania Press
Philadelphia, Pennsylvania 19104-4011

Library of Congress Cataloging-in-Publication Data
Roustang, François.
[Comment faire rire un paranoïaque? English]
How to make a paranoid laugh, or, What is psychoanalysis? /
François Roustang ; translated by Anne C. Vila.
p. cm. — (Critical authors & issues)
Includes bibliographical references and index.
ISBN 0-8122-3525-8 (cloth: alk. paper). —
ISBN 0-8122-1708-X (paper: alk. paper)
1. Psychoanalysis—Philosophy. 2. Individuation (Psychology)
3. Psychotherapist and patient. I. Title. II. Title: How to make
a paranoid laugh. III. Title: What is psychoanalysis. IV. Series.
RC506.R68513   1999
616.89′17—dc21   99-36953
                                                        CIP

Contents

Preface

You'll undoubtedly think that the question embodied in the main title of this book is meant to be amusing.[1] You're not wrong in that assumption, given that we are, in the end, amused only by serious matters. The matter at hand is more serious than most, as you'll realize shortly. But it must make you smile at least, so that you'll allow yourself to be drawn in by it. This question is, in fact, at the heart of your existence as a human being in this culture and, even more obviously, at the heart of the practice of psychotherapists of every sort. It remains to be seen whether your merriment subsides when you begin to sense the repercussions of this question, and to be determined whether it annoys you when you see how much it implicates you. We can nonetheless draw some consolation from these defensive reactions, because the issue of the paranoid and the paranoid's laughter has been around for quite some time now. Freud claimed that he had "succeeded where the paranoid had failed." But Groddeck wrote to Ferenczi: "Let's hope that he hasn't forgotten how to laugh."[2] Those two colleagues could, while they were in top form at the beginning of the twentieth century, brandish their independent spirit. However, things deteriorated afterward, and each of them paid the price for his impertinence in his own way. Let us hope that the same thing doesn't happen here.

Why single out the figure of the paranoid? Because it is emblematic of our culture, and thus reveals to us the most refined condition that can be produced in the register of mental illness. Paranoia manifests itself first in the characteristics of the individual who adores himself and pushes away any mirror that does not reflect back a flattering image. Such an individual would like to have a therapy that narcissizes him. Paranoia is also responsible for instilling in us a crazy passion for control and mastery. Never to be disconcerted by life: that would be the culmination of the cure. Finally, paranoia reaches its peak in the need of a leader who has decided, before we have, what sort of knowledge is suitable for us. Never mind the damage that is done by subjecting people to such a situation. We are all budding paranoids who sustain ourselves through exasperated resentment or the expectation that we will achieve some sort of recognition and power, unless we are already fully formed paranoids, who lord it over everyone else in the pathetic little world they've managed to carve out for themselves. Under these conditions, if we want to seek out treatment and get to the source of what ails us, the paranoid within us must be treated.

But how? Through laughter. But what sort of laughter are we talking about, given that there are so many different kinds? Obviously, the ability to laugh at oneself. Why, one might ask, would that be a form of medicine? Despite its lightheartedness, this kind of laughter carries so much weight that it touches and accentuates the contours of everything that moves; it also pervades our realities, animating every part while strengthening what is weak and reducing pretension. It does not judge, doesn't impose anything, and is content to embrace what is while hoping to transform it little by little. With paranoia one had all the worst, whereas with laughter at oneself one has all the best: proximity as opposed to distance; the tolerance that comes through realism; finitude without despair; humanity, along with the uncertainty that sharpens the attention and fosters the chance discoveries of astonishment, as opposed to horror; and life rather than death. For laughter at oneself does not possess anything, it doesn't seize hold of anyone, and it doesn't panic over anything: it considers, and is amused. It is a way of saying, so I'm still here, after all; we'll see what happens tomorrow.

But how can you make a paranoid laugh at himself? That question does not have an easy answer, because this kind of laughter holds the greatest danger for him. It supposes the abolition of all of the defenses the paranoid has constructed to keep at bay his anxiety that his sense of self will dissolve. What the paranoid lacks are self-limits, which should have served their function without him having to worry about it. That is why he must borrow limits that turn out to be artificial and inevitably alienating. He needs to rely upon a counterforce, the force of his persecutor or the person who is assumed to be that, who will protect him from the risk of expanding himself, and who will trace a boundary that will allow him to reaffirm, at every moment, his certainty or illusion that he exists in a circumscribed space. Without such an enemy, he would collapse.

The paranoid's entourage was unable to establish relationships with him early on that would have made him distinct; that is why he has had to resort to makeshift solutions. Because the presence of others threatens him with intrusion, and their absence threatens him with the loss of his sense of self, he constructs thought systems that have no relation to reality, and he does everything he can to set them into operation. He is obsessed with his hatred for life because, lacking any self-limits, he believes that life can only invade him or pass him by. He becomes an abstraction himself. It is the impossibility of distinction that prompts his need for mastery. Incapable of feeling the primary sentiment of existence, he turns himself into the guarantor of truth. He can never be wrong. Because he is never at a proper distance, he cannot engage in the process of welcoming or rebuffing others, or control the rhythm of their advances and retreats. For him, there will never been any choice other than surrender or triumph in dealing with humans. In short, he is not an individual who is differentiated in and through his relations with others.

How would it be possible to make him laugh at himself, if we psychotherapists produced the same means of defending ourselves in the process? We appear to be immersed in such a vast ocean of certitudes concerning our profession, its practice, and its theories that we have difficulty perceiving any opening through which laughter at ourselves could be introduced. For us to be able to transmit this form of laughter we must accept a first requirement, one that might be formulated in these terms: we must cast doubt on all theoretical affirmations. The psychoanalyst or psychiatrist or psychotherapist who asserts that something is definitively sure in the order of intellectual construction can only play the paranoid's game. The paranoid confines himself, in fact, to the register of abstraction—the abstraction of the system and of its operation. To avoid ever having to leave that register he will incite opposition in this regard. A paranoid—and the obsessional or hysterical patient are oftentimes not far removed—will, for example, try to find out what the psychotherapist might have said or written; he will try to perceive what his therapist holds to be theoretical evidence and will, indeed, easily detect it in his lucid madness. And he will attack this crucial point, sure of touching his interlocutor in his weak spot. If the therapist feels wounded by those remarks or shows any resistance whatsoever, even by remaining silent in order to protect what belongs to him, the paranoid will not fail to take advantage of it in order to avoid the risk of being put into question himself. If, by contrast, the therapist can make fun of and in himself, and laugh at what he defends in public, in private, or within himself, the paranoid will enter into a state of anxiety that is necessary to trigger the collapse of his defenses, which were sustained through the resistance of the therapist. The therapist's ability to laugh wholeheartedly at his own convictions and certitudes thus seems to be the first condition for easing the symptoms of the paranoid. What the paranoid is going to come up against—without, precisely, being able to confront—is the passion of disbelief that must fill the therapist. This is not a forbidden kind of disbelief, but an easy-going, practical one that can undo at any moment all preliminary assumptions. This sort of disbelief would, for example, entail not brandishing generalized lack of meaning as another absolute—that would lead back to paranoia— but rather cautiously demonstrating the proposed meanings and making their inadequacy evident.

In order for the paranoid's laugh to make itself heard, we must respond to yet another requirement, one that is correlative to the first. In fact, although the therapist should give no support to the paranoia, he must at the same time make its expression possible, for fear of seeing the paranoid become dispersed because he lacks limits to contain his madness. The therapist must provide such limits for the paranoid. But where can those limits be found? Because they can no longer be situated in the beliefs the paranoid has forged for himself out of desperation, they will have to be discovered in a different register. But what then is this thing that is going to be proposed in order to give the paranoid limits—or more precisely, a sense of distinction that can in no way be transformed into mastery? In the opposite case, the paranoia will seize the occasion and feed on it. For the paranoid to be able to laugh, it can happen only through the intermediary of the therapist's ability to laugh at himself; that laughter must, however, serve as proof that everything is still holding together at a time when, in the mind of the paranoid, nothing is holding together any more.

The therapist's laughter must be a support that has no support, a foundation that cannot be established, an assurance that resists the most radical criticism and, above all, defies every attempt to capture it definitively. Certainly, it is something elementary that is accepted without reflection, something that is indispensable but unrecognized: a vital breath whose rhythm remains mysterious, an aroma of tranquillity, a light that traces the contours, the pure capacity for moving, a totally occupied place—in short, the force of a complex presence, a presence that is our common destiny and that we all overlook even as we entrust ourselves to it.

To forestall any knowing smiles that might be inspired by the ideas I've just evoked, I will return to an example that I have already mentioned. A paranoid wanted to provoke his therapist's opposition by making more and more caustic remarks about his furniture, his voice, his words, or his writings. The therapist did not react to these remarks. So, without realizing it, the paranoid carried with him the most unpleasant odors: he sweated in clothes that had not been taken to the dry cleaner, he put on the most acrid colognes, and he deliberately stepped on dog droppings. The strongest deodorizers and repeated efforts to air out the room could not overcome this pestilence. It started to subside, however, to the point of disappearing, the minute the therapist figured out the game. What this man, who wanted to be cured, was trying to do was stir up an opposition that would be inevitable but could produce no form of protest. Without knowing it—and it was essential that he not be aware of this—he was asking a decisive question: Is my odor, the odor of my illness, bearable? That is, can the dialogue of odors be established and thereby give me some form of the elementary limit I've always been missing?

This is an exemplary case, because the paranoid is better versed than anyone in constructing defenses. He is thus capable of ripping off all masks, banning all equivocations, and disarming the hasty defenses that are produced by an overly rapid interpretation. But, with his hatred for life, he demands from the person who claims to be able to offer him a remedy the personal distinction that he lacks. In order to face the thrusts he makes, one must determine what remains true, solid, and incontestable at base, in the foundations of his being. It is the personal body that is put to the test—that is, the appropriation of his physical existence in relation to others. This is an opportunity for the therapist to reinhabit his space and learn all over again how to move around in it, leaving reflection aside or obliging it to concentrate in the interior, the center.

Although it is an exemplary case, it is not an unusual one. Haven't we all had a visitor who complained or rejoiced at the odor of the room where we receive our guests—the smell of the dust on the books, or that of the people who were just there? Should we rush to reply that there is nothing surprising in such remarks because they are the effect of transference? By invoking that big word, some people might think that they have put the matter to rest. Yet there remains at least one question to be addressed. The fact that the man in the example used odors to express his feelings regarding the therapist does not, in itself, explain why he chose that route. Some will undoubtedly reply: he did so because his words failed to attract the enemy he needed, so he had to resort to a means of existence and expression that exonerated him for any aggression, yet that nonetheless created an opposition that was beneficial for him. But, in that case, wasn't he simply reinventing the bases of his relations with other humans? He did not initially use odors as an instrument for expressing a relationship without using words. He was working at a more elementary level: he was constructing that instrument. That is, odors—and the same is true of the intonation of the voice, the quality of a gaze, the elegance of a gesture—provided him with the necessary distance, established mistrust or confidence, and marked the limits of the body.

What the paranoid invites us to do is to ask ourselves how the relational body is constituted. Like life, that body is formed through contact.[3] There is a story about a mother who was desperate because her newborn refused to eat and had to be taken to the hospital; the mother went to see the analyst Françoise Dolto. Dolto suggested that the mother wrap a scarf around her neck during the day and then place the scarf near her infant in the evening. The baby very soon rediscovered his need to eat. Perhaps the mother, by being intrusively solicitous, had smothered with affection the child she had just brought into the world, whereas her deferred scent reestablished the proper distance. Direct bodily contact would have been pernicious; the measured degree of tangible odor corresponded to the reactive force the child had at his disposal and succeeded in surrounding his body with a human and humanizing envelope. However mundane this story may be for ethicists, it gives us an important piece of information concerning the training of the personal body in the human being. Of course, odors are not the only senses that govern this training process: each of the senses that the culture has distinguished is involved, along with all of the interchanges that occur among the senses. A mother who interprets the different cries or whimpers of her child immediately and exactly, who perceives when he is happy or suffering, and who holds him close to soothe him, trains his body as a human being to take part in human communication. Thus, if transference is the index of the type of relationship an individual repeatedly establishes, one must trace back in time to determine how that relationship was instituted, and then remake it, when poorly formed, through the appropriate means. Those means consist essentially of the various figures of contact.

If this is the case, the question of knowing how an individual can enter into relation with another becomes meaningless. The personal body—the body that is humanly animated—is constituted by contact and does not exist without it. The personal body is and can be only a relational body—a social body, one might say. It exists only through relation, and there is no relation without it. It is distinct and distinguished by its personal envelope, but it would not have any personal envelope if the people around it and the environment had not constantly provided something in which it could wrap itself. Those people and that environment would in turn be nothing in themselves if they did not carry out the task of enveloping.

When we imagine a body that is not only endowed with autonomy—for it must, of course, be that—but also isolated to the point of lacking any dependency, then we are once again speaking of the point at which the human mind can detach itself through dreams or thought, the place where reflection escapes and closes upon itself, and where language no longer addresses anyone—the point, in other words, that borders on insanity. Some people consider this, and this alone, to be the site where individuation is carried out. It may, in fact, be possible to describe the human being in such terms, if one considers the possibility of madness to be the principle of its individual specificity! We must, however, admit that if we adopt such a point of view, there will be no hope of relieving the human condition of some of its weight; we can only get further and further entrenched in that perspective.

To heal certain wounds the personal body, which is at once the guarantor of individuation and the thing that enables a person to relate to things and people, must be brought back to the level of the sensations of contact that constitute it. What, in this context, is the attitude the therapist must assume both at the beginning and throughout the cure? Freud spoke of "floating attention." But attention to whom, and what? To words? Certainly. But should one be attentive to words alone? No, not at all. It is a question of paying attention to the patient as a total person. This means that the therapist must rediscover for himself the level that enables a human being to make the first formative contacts. It does not mean that he should analyze behavior, examine in detail what facilitates or hinders it, and consider what is said or hidden; rather, he should combine all of that into a single apprehension so as to reassemble and reduce the existence of his patient to what can be perceived through the humanized senses. It is important to consider the patient in his present singularity and describe solely his global existence: that is, to envelop him from the very start in the individuation he has achieved as a body, as a vital spirit, and as a mind. All of the senses—indeed, only the senses, in their transmodality—enter into play, because it is the senses that first make us human and that serve as the basis for communication, exchange, and contact. The foundation of positive or negative transference (assuming that we want to keep that word) might well be defined as refinement or lack of tact.

The term "equally floating attention," which Freud invented to define the analyst's initial attitude, proves that he saw this as the necessary condition for the success of the operation. He must have suspected that this was the only means of providing for the reformation of the personal body as an inhabited personal totality, and the only chance of making an eventual transformation possible.

On the other hand, what are we going to propose to the patient at the outset (and even if it is happening after several long detours, this will always take place at the outset, at the ground level)? Quite simply, that he be attentive to what he feels with his hands, in his feet, through his eyes, his ears, or his tongue; that he become absorbed in the rhythm of his breathing; that he get a clear sense of his place; in a word, that he be present to his body. We should tell him not to forget to make an initial contact with what is tangible as he tries to construct answers to the question *why*, but instead to put all the resources of his intelligence, his thought, and his speech at the service of his sensations. In other words, rather than elevating himself to the sphere of the subtleties of the mind, he should descend into the foundations of his own life.

What this entails is by no means a regression to the archaic or primitive level, to a stage that fosters confusion or symbiosis. On the contrary, the explanation of elementary life favors distinction. This is, therefore, not a return to some buried past, to an infantile state where nothing has been elaborated as yet, and one's humanity is uncertain. Rather, it is a process of acceding to personal unity through a fundamental renewal of everything that forms a differentiated individual—a withdrawal of the individual toward his constitutive parts.

By making the patient attentive to the sensations rather than to thoughts or emotions, one destroys the transference that could have developed. For what becomes primary is not the relation to the therapist, but the relation of the patient-agent to his own body—that is, to his own life. Instead of remaining fixated on the person of the therapist and reproducing through him the type of relation he has with everyone else, the patient concentrates on what he is through an echo effect created by the therapist's concentration; he reconstitutes his own limits through the contact and tact of the initiator, and thus individualizes himself further. This does not mean that the patient-agent is closed off within himself. Quite the contrary, by sharpening all of his senses he opens up for himself the field of all possible relations. Within that field, the psychotherapist becomes no more than one among many, a person who is necessary today for the apprenticeship that is under way but who will be useless tomorrow, when the habit of concentration has become second nature. It is easy for the patient to detach himself from the therapist because, by endeavoring himself to stay at the level of contact without any further elaboration, the therapist has reinforced the distinction of the patient-agent and thus made him freer to act with the same indifference or interest toward the therapist as toward any other thing or person.

*   *   *

My remarks on the two conditions required for the paranoid to be able to laugh at himself were designed to introduce the chapters that follow. There are, in fact, two concerns that pervade these essays: first, a desire to avoid taking for granted any of the concepts that are standardly accepted in the field of psychoanalysis or psychotherapy, and second, a wish to describe more precisely the relational experience that can bring about modifications in existence. In reality, these pages, written over the course of fifteen years, are marked not by two concerns but by one and one alone. Because I was unable to escape the insistent question of change and the conditions it requires, I concluded that the answers that had thus far been proposed to the question were insufficient.

Why, I wondered, did the notable improvements in patient health that had sometimes been achieved through the analytic cure evade every effort to explain them? Why, in all too many cases, did therapy produce no benefit, and why was it quite often the scene of persistent deteriorations? It was impossible to reassure myself by considering that a cure is a bonus in psychoanalysis, that it should not be pursued as a goal, and that I should, therefore, not dwell on it but rather undertake more captivating theoretical tasks.

Having admitted that, my work had only begun. The reader will note that the basic questions (What happens in psychoanalysis? Why doesn't anything happen in psychoanalysis? Why, even when one understands a problem, doesn't anything change?) did not lead to clear-cut answers. To move from there to a result with which I am satisfied today (but probably won't be tomorrow), I had to follow a complex progression. I can, nonetheless, retrace some of its steps in retrospect. The themes on which I touch in these essays are richly interconnected. However, for the sake of clarity, I shall try to deduce them from each other in a more or less logical manner.

One question stood out over all the rest: What was the status of the so-called psychoanalytic theory? Seeking not to describe this theory but to situate it, a good many authors, who do not hide their admiration for the work of Freud, have answered that it is quite simply a mythology—a grandiose mythology, no doubt, given that it will soon be the only one to outlive the twentieth century, but a mythology even so. For my part, I had reached this conclusion, without having sought it in any way, through a patient and minutely detailed study of Freud's style. One day, I had the impression that I had grasped precisely how the warp and the weft of

Freud's writing were interwoven. Once I had found that, all it took was pulling on a single thread for the entire fabric to unravel—not as a work of art, but as a message of truth.

It was inevitable that I should draw some conclusions from this observation. For example, if there is no psychoanalytic theory, only a mythology, there can be no question of using such a theory as a guide in the progress of a cure. It is impossible and dangerous to try to make a cure fit a mythology, because the latter is supposed to be explicative or consoling; it can under no circumstances serve as a rule for action. The only thing that can do that is a technique, whose failures or successes cannot go beyond a generalization. If, as a side effect of analysis, a person abandons his beliefs and adopts as true the beliefs proposed by this mythology, all that can be produced is a surface change: the old beliefs have been traded in for others that are simply easier to maintain because they conform more closely to the intellectual trends of the day. I was thus obliged to look elsewhere to find the ins and outs of an authentic modification.

To that end, I had to ask myself how existence might open onto a different future. Temporal regression, which had been proposed as the magic word that would lift all symptoms, seemed to result in constructions that might be intellectually satisfying but were incapable of serving as an instrument of transformation. It consequently became futile to look for causes in the past, because what the past held was not, properly speaking, causes, but merely eventual motifs or reasons, whereas the psychoanalyst had to find the means of unleashing the forces that could renew a patient's mode of relation to things and to people.

It was long maintained that free speech—that is, the kind that is produced without any specific intention or wish—was necessary to accomplish this. Free speech was deemed to be the only thing that could provide access to the world of phantasms and dreams, that wellspring in which, as romanticism taught us, the sources of creation are hidden. That belief also highlighted the possibility of madness, commonly seen in our culture as the most obvious trait specific to the human race. With time, however, this way of thinking about the curative process no longer seemed indispensable.

Following the work of Michel Henry, who proposed a radical distinction between representation and affect,[4] one needed merely to stay at the level of affect, most particularly affect in the form of anxiety, in order to apprehend the forces of life—not only sexual forces, but those that propel the human being to strive for possession, power, and strength. It became apparent later that it was not enough simply to apprehend these forces: one had to appropriate them as well. Hence the importance that was progressively accorded to the exercise of decision during therapy: namely, the patient's decision to recognize his state and his suffering, to stop lamenting them as if they stemmed from an ineluctable fate, but rather to take responsibility for them in every respect—in other words, to invest his existence such as it is today and draw upon it, the better to transform it tomorrow. For all it takes to allow the forces of life to operate is to settle into the place where one is, without neglecting anything.

Hence the discovery of hypnosis, which Freud, contrary to common belief, never abandoned, and which he quite often used as the motor of a cure and, in many forms, as its solution. For my part, I discovered that although it took the appearance of a kind of sleep that liberates us from our usual preoccupations, hypnosis was in fact a hypervigilance, a paradoxical wakefulness that provides access to all of the parameters that constitute human life.[5] Because it frees us from worrying about staying in control, hypnosis leads us into a state in which we are receptive to existence such as it is and, through that, to a singularization that can operate in secret.

This rediscovery was the main result of my ongoing reflection on transference, or at least on the enigmas of the relation that is established in analysis; the reader will be able to see my efforts to probe that subject through the inevitable repetitions that occur in these pages. The psychoanalyst's role could not, I concluded, be reduced to a single function, nor could he confine himself to the position of the person who is supposed to know all, or finally, serve as a pure desire without object. His person entered into play, and could not avoid doing so. That, of course, raised some difficult questions. In any case, what was at stake for the analysand was his access to his identity—or to his sense of distinction in his relationship to things or beings, which amounts to the same thing— an access that could be one of the ways of defining a cure.

For a long time, I considered the psychoanalyst's uncertainty about his own identity to be a necessity for allowing the identity of the analysand to come to light; it was as if the analyst was betting his own card in the relationship and, because he was un-

certain himself, needed the analysand's certainty and thereby had
to desire and produce it. Thanks to the practice of self-hypnosis,
which allowed the psychoanalyst to take his own place by invest-
ing his own humanized body, his interlocutor could be invited to
take his own distinct place in all relations. The analyst's uncertainty over his own identity therefore took on a different meaning:
by taking his place in its fullest sense, the analyst was forced to
accept every aspect of his limits and his misery and thus to rediscover, in a different mode, the benefits of uncertainty. Taking one's
place supposes that one has given up trying to represent any ideal,
and that one has abandoned all illusions about oneself. Although
it was impossible to avoid the generalized disillusion that accom-
panied this conclusion, I faced that disillusion without despair, in
the lighthearted elation of laughing at myself.

Le Thou, July 1995

Chapter 1
Nobody

One day in 1892, the patient whom Freud had just cured of her ills threw her arms around his neck. This action prompted him to realize something that he had long suspected: "This gesture could not be the effect of my charms. It is not meant for me." From this realization was born the idea of transference—that "false relationship," as Freud initially called it with unmatched precision. Transference is thus supposed to be like a love letter whose address has been lost. It is supposed to be the result of a subtraction: the psychotherapist as a particular person slips away and allows himself to be put in the place of the patient's Other, the Other that constitutes her, inseparably, and that she loves today but may detest tomorrow. Therefore, transference is love insofar as it is directed at nobody, because it is directed at one's Other—a protean, unstable, but imperious image.

This Other that constitutes me is formed by the convergence and interpenetration of the images, people, events, or things with which I have identified, with which I have sought to identify, or with which I could not help identifying—in short, by everything that marks my history, whether I know it or not, all of the particularities that have created me as a new mixture, inevitably distinct from the other individuals in my species. However, these more or less unified images, which may be figures, accidents, or objects, do more than compose the history of my distinction. Inasmuch as they have become my indelible Other, they definitively mark my future; they can, moreover, compose the image of my destiny as I perceive it, because I will never be able to avoid having been formed in this manner and having my future determined by it.

Transference is the projection of this Other onto the analyst. It is widely recognized that, over the course of a cure, the psychoanalyst is prompted to don the variety of masks to which this Other is attached—that is, to assume successively the multiple positions with which the patient must grapple in order to exist. Through this Nobody, the patient encounters the Other to whom he is permanently tied and who forces him to repeat certain incessant patterns of acting, thinking, and relating to others; any success the patient has in ridding him- or herself of this Other, in ceasing to be its paralyzed victim, is, it seems, illusory. The psychoanalyst thus takes on the role of the fixed figure of the patient's destiny. This Nobody is, quite simply, the being who keeps the patient in prison. Rather than opening up for him or her the real possibilities offered by a path she or he has never taken, every new identification that is conjured up sends the patient back to the same chains and the same circular efforts.

The hysteric—and, undoubtedly, not only her or him—swiftly embraces the turn that analysis takes under such circumstances. Nobody, who says nothing, knows a great deal about the patient; indeed, he knows everything, everything that is going to happen to the patient, everything that cannot help happening to him. Of course, the patient generally grants Nobody such knowledge, for Nobody is a great scholar, a perspicacious and audacious being who has so many things to reveal to the world. Yet all of his bluster barely hides the certainty that constrains the patient: from the height of his knowledge, he holds written everything that the patient is, everything that he will become, all of the possible possibles. And, if the patient truly wants his pronouncements to be more than bluster, he will turn himself into an object of study, living matter for his knowledge, an object of extreme suffering capable of unveiling to him the ultimate secrets, the kind that are deciphered within the bodies of sacrificial victims that have been cut open by an augur.

It is in this manner that, against a backdrop of loss and fragmentation, love is born for the Other—an Other who is totalitarian, demanding, insatiable, and devouring, and whose power, glory, and universal knowledge the patient endeavors to establish. The patient, however, seeks to construct the Other in order to demolish him, because love is also hate and because, if the patient offers herself as a victim to the Other, the Other must pay with his life for sacrificing the patient. The hysteric, as is well known, only accepts a master, or invents the master she accepts, in order to rob him of his strength and ridicule him in his nudity and impotence. It may be, however, that psychoanalysts avoid drawing the conclusions suggested by this phenomenon.

Supposedly, therefore, transference-love marks the end of the analysis. By asking for love, the patient supposedly puts an end to the psychoanalytic process: refusing to use transference as a device for addressing Nobody, he or she is able to recall the identifications that have formed her or him and thus is able to unravel or reconnect them in a way that is less constraining. But what if, as was suggested earlier, it turns out that transference produces the hysteric (this possibility has been raised but not properly explored)? In other words, what if the transference to which one holds so rigidly, because one is Nobody and won't move a inch from that position, ineluctably produced a state of paralysis, an object of science, and thus an implacable determinism? If, even when the opposite result was sought, the convergence of identifications onto the analyst turned him into a new version of the Furies who viewed any escape from repetition as a form of hubris, then transference-love could have a function other than that of putting an end to the analysis.

What if, for example, this love aimed to make the analysis possible, in the sense that analysis implies a transformation of the relationship to time and the opening up of new possibilities? After all, seducing the Furies, those falsely "benevolent" beings, would not be such a bad idea, and arousing in them an emotion that predominates in mortals could make them abandon their vengeful preoccupation with the law. Why wouldn't the hysteric try to upset the impeccable posture of the analyst, whom she supposes knows everything, and who has ended up believing himself to be wise or all-knowing, unless he is even more constrained by the vulnerability of his doubt or ignorance?

That answer is not so easy, however. Many patients (if not all) settle fervently into the grips of a double impossible condition and try to enclose the analyst in it as well. The analyst is thrown back and forth from one wall to the other like a squash ball until he is exhausted: "If you don't answer, you're a bastard, because you're dropping me without doing anything—you're unmoved, unconcerned, cynical, and a con artist on top of that; but if you answer, you're an idiot, because you haven't understood that this is a game that I want neither to win nor lose: all I care about is staying in motion." Although the patient cannot bear it when the psychoanalyst resists, he or she turns away from the analyst who has caved in.

Does this mean that the room for maneuvering is narrow? Perhaps, but it is not clear that the question must be put in those terms. One would have to have a clear sense that the offer or request for love in therapy was initially made as a means of obscuring another question: Am I, or am I not, subject to destiny? Or to ward off this obsessive fear: Can I ever escape from repetition? Only fools believe Virgil's saying that "Love conquers all." For the hysteric, love is a challenge made to everyone in general, and most especially to Nobody, the Other who never stops tormenting her with his perfection, his fullness, his sufficiency. The hysteric is made from this Other because she is perfect, total and free of wounds, but she doesn't want to know anything about the Other because she wants to shape him; as a consequence, she cannot stand this Nobody who sends that image back to her. She is going to love Nobody in order to disturb the surface of that mirror; but, if it gets disturbed, she will turn away with her most sardonic laugh, unless that disturbance is the first stage of a breach, an opening, an uncertain image that would be tolerable for her if it were tolerable for him.

It is a mistake to think that the hysteric who offers love is asking for it in return. She says that she is asking for it, except that she does not want it. This leads us to think that she wants to lure the analyst out of his position, make him fall in love and manifestly so; yet, if she succeeds, she once again restores the place he had occupied, returns him to it, or assigns to it another of the same type. We should understand that although she needs the figure of her destiny—that is, the figure of her perfection, her omnipotence, and her unalterable agitation—she also wants to be finished with that figure. She does not know what she wants, because she no longer wants what she wants. She does not ask for love, that softening of the irreparable; rather, she asks that the enchanted circle be broken, or, as Jules Michelet would put it, that she cease to be the sorceress of this science,[1] and thus that the analyst stop being Nobody but that he not be in love either. In other words, *her love is a request not for love, but for implication.*

What can implicating oneself mean for a psychoanalyst? First of all, the reflexive form of the verb is not appropriate here, because the psychoanalyst is implicated whether he wants to be or not, and he need only produce no new act in order to be so. He should be content to recognize—but recognize what? Precisely, that he is involved in some way in this situation. Not in the sense that he is responsible for the form that the ending of the analysis takes, because what matters when that alarm signal or stop sign appears is to interpret it correctly. The ending of the analysis lies not in the love that is offered (that is only its symptom), but in the fact that the analyst believes that he is Nobody, takes himself to be the pure reflection of the Other that constitutes the patient, and claims, in a word, not to be involved in any way. If implication is an act, it consists for the analyst in maintaining an indelible relationship between himself and Nobody. He is not altogether Nobody, or, in any case, he is not Nobody as anyone at all might be: rather, he is Nobody as somebody. For Odysseus, we'll recall, Nobody (*Nemo* in Greek) was a name—that is, a proper name. Simply recognizing this has the effect of telling the patient, "I am not altogether your Other; rather, I surreptitiously entered into the mirror, and I've even modified its silver coating." Implicating oneself—and here the reflexive form becomes appropriate once more—thus seems to mean displacing oneself slightly and slipping another figure underneath the figure of Nobody, who had been presented to the other as his or her Other.

This shift is decisive for relativizing the uniqueness of transference and for undercutting the monolithic nature of the entity who supposedly knows and determines the future. There is no longer a full image, that of Nobody, and next to it, at a certain distance, the limited image of that entity; for the gap between the two would inevitably have a qualitative effect on the image of Nobody, who is no longer exclusively Nobody because he is particularized in the person of the analyst. In simple terms, this would be put as follows: if I perceive that my analyst is speaking for himself and no longer in function of me alone, then I can no longer consider him to be my reflection or projection, and I must admit that he is distorting me. But, if he is distorting me—he who, just a short while ago, I took to be Nobody, my pure Other—then there is no Nobody; the Other that constitutes me will never be pure and omnipotent and true, and there will never be anything but others and just enough of Nobody to keep these others from falling into pieces. There are differences, diversity, relative factors, and perhaps even relations. Nobody is not the law.

But what grief this would cause! Grief, first of all, for the patient, who can undoubtedly be called here—and here alone—an analysand, because he or she destroys the transference. There is grief on the other side too, of course. Take, for example, the following off-the-cuff remarks made by an analyst who is a media celebrity:

"It still happened, on occasion, that I thought about myself while I was listening to a patient."

"What did that mean?"

"That my own analysis had not been completed. We are nothing when we are listening to our patient. We're an object-subject that is indispensable for transference. Everyone knows that today."

Obviously, in her practice this analyst does something quite different from what she claims to do; for there may be no one more implicated than herself in her cures, and that is what makes her so brilliant. This does not, however, prevent her from applying to herself here the official doctrine on transference, a doctrine that we would be well advised to critique. For when one says that one is nothing and that one has discarded one's self, one obviously makes oneself everything and settles out of range, in a state of omnipotence that leads directly to transforming psychoanalysis into a substitute for religion.

We are no longer back in the days of Freud. The question of transference—and consequently, the question of transference-love—could not be put in the same terms or framed according to the same foundations. In order for the invention of transference to be effectively followed, an ideal had to be set: the absent psychoanalyst. That ideal was necessary in order to single out the fact that all relations are established on the basis of a phantasmatization of the other as my Other, as the Other that constitutes me. This was thus a limiting description whose purpose was to fix and activate a universal mechanism. Wanting the psychoanalyst to be absent is, in a sense, tantamount to affirming the condition of possibility for studying processes of phantasms and dreams in which one never has any Other beside oneself. However, moving from this transcendental operation to practice, and making it appear that the psychoanalytic cure can unfold according to this type of epistemological purity, is an entirely different affair, one that produces confusion. The mere fact that the psychoanalyst mimics absence does not permit us to conclude that he is truly absent. Those who seek, moreover, to convince us that the sufficient condition for the psychoanalyst's absence is his own psychoanalysis, and that it allows him to set aside his self, definitely turn the psychoanalyst into a charlatan and a con artist. One might even say that it is here that the major fraud perpetrated by psychoanalysis lies. For if the psychoanalyst could really make himself absent, he would escape from the rules of any relationship in which the other functions as an Other because he is an Other that the other party has fabricated; he would be a sorcerer, a king, or a god. This amounts to doing what bad politicians, petty priests, and lovers do: equating the function and the operator.

The fact that this confusion may lie at the heart of psychoanalytic practice—and in a certain sense, constitute its very mainspring—does not justify viewing it naively as the supreme form of clarity or as evidence that one must accept uncritically. If we raise this confusion to the status of law, it can only lead us to abdicate our duty to address the problems posed by the end of analysis. Doing away with transference begins by refusing the received ideas that surround it, because they are designed to shield the psychoanalyst from questions about what he does and what he triggers. Establishing as a principle that the analyst is absent allows him, in fact, to make himself absent. And, to get back to the question of transference-love, that is what the hysteric cannot tolerate. She knows that the resolution of transference is tied to the way in which transference is conceived. She does not want to stop the analysis; rather, she wants to raise the question of the beginning of its end.

Thus the question of transference-love is, perhaps, just as poorly framed as is that of transference. This love only prompts the end of the analysis if it is misinterpreted by the analyst—that is, interpreted as a request for love when it should be considered as an opportunity that arises at a certain moment in the analysis for the analyst to displace himself, to create a distance between his function and his position, by implicating himself. For the hysteric, transference-love may be essentially a way—roundabout, at first— to reveal the double bind that chains her to her Other, so that she can at last exorcize this figure from her destiny. In sum, this love may be the first in a series of tentative steps on the path toward the relative and the possible, even if it is improbable that those steps will become reality.

If it is recognized that the hysteric is asking for the analyst's implication, as we defined it earlier, she will no longer be at fault. She will only appear to be a guilty seductress to the extent that the analyst seeks to blind himself to his desire—not his Desire with a capital *D*, that is, a pure desire of pure desire, but a particular desire, one that is tied to a particular image of his Other. If she loves, it is also as a means of being liberated from that guilt, which arises from the fact that she alone would be responsible for the desire. That, after all, is what she is accused of being. (Here, psychoanalysis is merely repeating commonplaces that are as old as Mediterranean civilization.) If the analyst implicates himself—that is, if he becomes relative and partial, and ceases to represent her Other in the guise of the law—then she will be able to fantasize without guilt that she is making love with him. Not acting out that fantasy will mean that she has made a choice, that she has recognized that she is dealing with both the person of the analyst and a person fantasized in transference, rather than having come up in exasperation against an interdiction that never presents itself for what it is.

Interdictions can be seen as providing the person who invents them with a convenient, purified, and magnified expression of the impossibility of coexisting with his desire and taking responsibility for it. When we assume that the key aspect of desire is the relationship to the law, aren't we simply reassuring those who do not want to be hampered in pursuing their so-called "civilizing" efforts? Perhaps interdictions are established not to create desire, but to push it aside and pretend that it doesn't exist, which is a kind of defense commonly used by fathers and men to protect their power and trap women in the infernal cycle of guilt and impossibility. Lacan even went so far as to call this impossibility the highest tribunal the human being must face. This is not a theory but a description of a state of fact—the perverse montage of inhumanity that is constantly revived by politicians, paranoids, and scholars to make those who oppose their projects feel guilty. Transference-love may be nothing but one of the many attempts that have been made to weaken the countless certitudes promoted by those figures.

Chapter 2
Uncertainty

It is not doubt but certainty that makes people crazy.
Nietzsche

It seems that doubt is not possible, if we adopt the point of view of biology. Isn't Darwinism based on the incontestable fact that small differences exist among the individuals within a single species?[1] Why isn't the same thing true in the field of sociology or psychology? Why do we invariably note an uncertainty in human beings, the torment of having to distinguish oneself from one's peers or conversely, the irrepressible need to blend into the crowd? The difference that man needs in order to maintain his existence is something he fears to the greatest degree. As a consequence, his individuality never seems able to be stable. The traditional question, "What is the principle of individuation?" and the more recent historical question, "When and in what context does Western individualism appear?" are, perhaps, formulations designed to distract us from a more agonizing question: first, what does the fact of humanity introduce that keeps the reality of individual differences from becoming definitively established; and second, what is it about this fact that unleashes the uncertainty of distinction and, as a product of uncertainty, threats that loom over existence itself?

Psychoanalysis would classically and confidently respond to the traditional and historical formulations of this question by maintaining that the singularity of the individual is grounded in the recollection of his history, which is always unique. By appropriating or reappropriating for himself the events and relationships that governed his birth and development, the patient restores or institutes his individuality. Up to now, he was the powerless victim of his past, manipulated by mechanisms of which he was not aware and over which he could consequently have no influence. Because he is in many ways a stranger to himself, he is susceptible to seeing himself in an image that, until now, has been fabricated by other people or other facts. He can henceforth recover his fundamental alterity, his difference, and recognize himself in it. He is no longer an automaton; he is now a distinct living being.

Things may not be as simple as that. The difficulties Freud encountered in his practice are well known. The work of recollection may not give the expected results; the symptoms may reappear and shift place. Moreover, recollection itself is often stopped by the force of transference, which the patient does not in the least wish to escape. As Freud notes, the patient swaps his neurosis for a neurosis of transference: that is, he reconstitutes his symptoms in function and by virtue of his relationship to the analyst. Far from developing a sense of distinction, he enters into a state of increased dependence that may give him the illusion of existence; in reality, he is mimicking the analyst and becoming his colorless double. Or the patient may be a chatterbox who does not know how to use his own words and who repeats psychoanalytic discourse, unless he turns into a fanatic over some cause.

In other words, it is not so easy to become "the subject of one's own history"; more exactly, one can only become such a subject, according to the most classical doctrine, through recourse to transference. But it is there, precisely, that all of the problems begin. For the relational force that is supposed to bring about separation, distinction, and individuation is also the force that works against those processes. This is not the place to explore that point in detail. Yet, given that transference can be considered as a paradigm that is quite well isolated from any relationship, we should try to say something about it. It might open up some new perspectives.

Psychoanalysts are not very fond of speaking about transference as a force, because that notion becomes obscure when it is imported from physics or mechanics into the psychic field, where it is no longer measurable; measurability, in fact, is the only thing that could make the concept of force clear and effective. However, one has no choice but to use this notion if one wants to account for the effects of analysis. It is not enough to repeat the commonly asserted idea that psychoanalysis is a process of speech; for although that might be what makes psychoanalysis original, it is not the source of its effectiveness. If speech is operative, it is only because it is situated in transference and is upheld by it; this is, therefore, where speech draws its force. In the past, Lacan asserted that a decisive distinction exists between empty speech and full speech,[2] but he did so with the intention of reducing everything, ultimately, to speech and of rejecting any attempt to conceive of the reality of the relationship that is established between the analyst and the analysand. These two domains of speech are separated precisely by the influence they exert, or don't exert, on transference as a specific relationship. It is not true that psychoanalysis operates through speech alone, or that speech alone is capable of instituting the break that is necessary to the existence of an individuated subject. Practitioners know this: it is in and through transference that the patient, projecting the elements of his history upon the analyst, can see them appear and by using those elements on, for, and against the analyst is able to appropriate them for himself. Speech is merely the medium that allows transference to take effect, develop, and be modified. However, for the patient to dare to reveal this story and shape it he must, to recall one of Freud's terms, be in a state of expectation[3] regarding the analyst—a pure expectation of the other, as an other. Conversely, the analyst must be in a state of expectation in regard to the patient, an expectation and confidence that arouse him in his subjectivity. These reciprocal expectations, which have no definite object, no external task to accomplish, and no social referent, provide a first definition of the relational force that constitutes the human individual, a force that they intensify to the extreme.

How can we further define this force, whose ambivalence is one of its most striking characteristics? Expectation can, in fact, change very quickly into a reciprocal dependence that may lead all the way to a need for the life—and thus the death—of the other. What this shows is that expectation is, in essence, the purified force of romantic passion, which, in its desire for union, is what simultaneously gives life and extinguishes it, what creates me through the other and nullifies me in him. During a "Wednesday Evening Gathering" in January 1907, Freud said:

There is only one power capable of overcoming resistances, and that is transference. We force the patient to renounce his resistances *out of love for us*. Our treatments are treatments accomplished through love. Our only remaining task is to eliminate the *personal* resistances (resistances to transference). We can heal for as long as the transference endures; the analogy with hypnosis treatment is striking. The only difference is that psychoanalysis uses the power of transference to bring about a *durable* change in the patient, whereas hypnosis is merely a skillful trick.[4]

This statement is explicit and clear. Yet we should add that this sort of love is particular, that it is not hindered by any social visibility, and that it carries with it no injunction other than subjective modification. It is an experiment in love in vitro. Freud would later return to this aspect of analysis when speaking of "transference-love."[5] But he was, by then, quite behind the times in comparison to the positions that had been taken by his close friends. He was wary about love in analysis—so wary that he no longer mentioned transference when he tried to account for the driving force that underlies the unification of groups; he compared the amorous state not to transference, but to hypnosis (and avoided suggesting their proximity). Between the amorous state and hypnosis, he wrote, there exists a fundamental difference: the latter "excludes sexual satisfaction."[6]

This obvious exclusion is worth lingering over. It may conceal some serious problem that is trying to avoid open expression. Wondering why psychoanalysts must renounce the sexual end of the love they inspire may seem downright incongruous; the most elementary code of professional ethics requires us to respect the wishes of the patient who comes to see us in order to be relieved of his symptoms, not to find a sexual partner. But that professional response is valid in many other cases; moreover, it does not account for the contradiction inherent to a treatment that leads to love but refuses its consequences. A second justification for excluding sexual satisfaction relies on the fact that carrying out one's desires would compromise the continuation of the treatment. How can someone dream, associate, and project on the basis of an other who has become a real persona, who is no longer a vague figure capable of representing many other people? This explanation, too, has its merits, but once again it posits that the exclusion of sexual satisfaction protects this love without clarifying its nature. Moreover, it is not so sure that, in this particular case, the sexual relationship would diminish the intensity of the liaison (as generally seems to be true); for what is created on the scene of the phantasm is difficult to refute by invoking reality. We are operating here in a strange register.

There is, in fact, a very special interdiction that weighs upon the psychoanalytic relationship. To understand it we need only recall one of the most typical aspects of any analysis. In transference, the psychoanalyst effectively becomes for the analysand his father or his mother, his sister, brother, or some close acquaintance, on the basis of traits that are minimal, trivial, or insignificant in themselves; in the analyst's office, the analysand recognizes the odor of a first house, hears its sound or its music, or finds the color of a landscape from his childhood. In short, if the analysand falls in love here (sometimes without knowing it), if that love is intense and violent to such a degree, and if its flip side—hate—can become terrible here, the reason is that all of those places, those characters, those characteristics, and those details belong to his first intimacies. What the analysand loves in the analyst, with an intensity he has never felt since childhood, are the faces of those who were sexually forbidden for him. The force of transference, the force of the love that can heal, is once again an unmatched and unmatchable passion; it is, however, a passion that works so secretly that the analysand is no longer aware of it, and it is marked by an interdiction on sexual relations—that is, by the incest prohibition. There is thus no need to refer to the exclusion of sexual satisfaction as an ethical rule or technique. This exclusion is inscribed in transference-love as the internal contradiction that gives it its specific quality. For an analyst and patient to act upon their sexual desires would, therefore, be not merely and above all a moral fault or a practical error, it would also entail the sexual taboo par excellence. But if such a thing happened, there would be no grounds for taking offense or reproving it either; one should not even be surprised, for it would simply be the manifestation of the force that had been set into play.

An opposite consequence should be drawn from this. If the transference is simply reactualized incest, and if the interdiction that weighs upon the psychoanalytic relationship reproduces the incest prohibition, then the driving force of the psychoanalytic cure—the force that is in operation, and that no one knew how to define—can be described as a new version of incestuous desire, the desire that governs the birth of every human individual. This desire may also be the prototype of all desire. Lacan accustomed us to conceiving of desire in terms that were designed to be as far removed as possible from the detestable notion of object relations and the ideas of gratification, frustration, adaptation, and self-sacrifice it suggests. Lacan's enterprise was to understand desire as having no object, as something that can only sustain itself through a lack or through an object that is fleeting. But isn't that just an abstract, remote, and disembodied way of referring obliquely to incestuous desire without really talking about it? In Lacan's theory, the prohibited object is changed in the absence of an object; and the object that is made inaccessible by the prohibition associated with it becomes something purely impossible. It is as if it were unbearable for the object to be forbidden; so, rather than having to work with and around the object in this singular situation, Lacan turned away from it by forging a celestial theory: he no longer wanted to see the object, so he erased it and marked its place with a hole or an outline. Given that, it is not surprising that some people come to regard psychoanalysis as part of a religious or mystical tradition in which a mysterious masochism combines with a logic gone haywire. This approach provides a means of avoiding a good deal of nonsense, but also a number of hindrances; it becomes unnecessary, for example, to assign psychoanalysis a precise goal in culture and society, which is required by the act of unmasking desire as the desire for prohibited incest. For that takes us back to the condition of possibility for the political and the social, and thus for the individual within those spheres. Thus conceived, transference approximates very closely the moving forces of education—if one is seeking not to create standardized individuals but rather beings capable of modification—and, for the same reasons, the moving force of the political sphere. This force that constantly tends toward realization (which is forbidden, on the penalty of returning to the state of fetal indistinction and negating the differentiation produced by time) is the primary source of all individuation, inasmuch as it is diverted from the inaccessible object and deferred from that realization toward other, larger objects. Isn't this a way, free from all forms of idealism, to reinvigorate the Freudian hypothesis of the libido as the first principle of human existence?

We must, however, recognize that when he invented transference, Freud viewed it above all as an instrument that would allow the analyst to maintain a maximum distance and thus avoid feeling involved or implicated in his own sexuality; this concept turns the psychoanalyst into a pure, unfeeling receptor or a pure mirror that is never disturbed. Transference is just as easily something else: it is the site that is purified, tightened to the point of passion, where the force of incestuous desire is deployed, and which places the analysand—and the analyst—in a state of extreme contradiction. Awakening the desire for incest that, when diverted, must permit individuation to occur cannot be accomplished without posing a serious threat to individual differentiation, since this operation can always trigger the wish to disappear into the maternal bosom. This is undoubtedly what causes setbacks and aggravations of the analysand's symptoms. This is also what produces those analyses that never end, because the analysand cannot detach himself from the site where he has rediscovered his first loves—the most promising, or the most new for those who have not experienced them—even while he is theoretically protected from their excesses by the remote presence of the analyst. But on the other hand, if this desire is not awakened, the individual will never find the strength necessary not just to survive, but to live.

Transference could, therefore, be the reproduction of incest and of its prohibition. But is it truly a matter of incest? To clarify this a bit, we should distinguish the different degrees to which incestuous desire can be realized. When one refers to incest, in the strict sense of the term, one is describing sexual relations between parents and children: mother-son relations,[7] father-daughter relations, or relations between a brother and sister, and sometimes between cousins. Might there not be reason to speak as well of incest between parents and children of the same sex, that is, between a father and son or between a mother and daughter? Undoubtedly because incest is usually discussed only in terms of prohibition, or because this prohibition is said to be society's founding principle, the emphasis is placed on the thing that conditions the development of a group: sexual reproduction, which supposes the difference of the sexes. However, if one considers the sexual individual, one is obliged to observe that the difference of the sexes is a reality that is just as unstable as the individual himself. Just as incest can trigger and abolish individual difference, so can it trigger and abolish sexual differences.[8]

Incest can, however, also exist when a true sexual passion is maintained between parents and children through gazes, caresses, and body care that go on well beyond adolescence.[9] This is undoubtedly why a very well-known woman psychoanalyst makes it a rule for parents not to kiss their children. Such excessive statements at least have the benefit of showing that incest is so present in relationships that it must be contained through prohibitions that go all the way back to its origins.

Finally, the notion of incest can be extended to the desire for sexual relations, which is expressed in phantasms and in dreams. Here, the prohibition can only operate by means of the guilt and shame that lead the person to repress the phantasms and block out the dreams. That is not to say that these phantasms and dreams will not find a way of reappearing in the form of symptoms.

The existence of incestuous phantasms and dreams poses no problem for psychoanalysts. They readily admit, for example, that a little girl's desire to have a child with her father is a structuring element for her. If pushed, they will not be overly disturbed if in such phantasms or dreams their person is substituted for those of the parents or close relations. But they will think that the amorous states that are directed at them, and even more so, the seductions that could lead to the sexual act, are to be considered as foreign to the analysis or as tending to put an end to it; and they will defend themselves against this through every means available. They forget, however, that the different levels at which incest can appear are inseparable. If its realization is unthinkable, it cannot be fantasized or dreamed. We should even turn the proposition around and affirm that incest can only act as a structuring principle in the sphere of phantasms and dreams to the extent that its realization is conceivable. And "conceivable" means that it is on both sides, on the side of the father or mother and the side of the children, and in analysis, on the side of the psychoanalyst and the side of the analysand.

These statements are scandalous but nonetheless extremely banal. The scandal that some want to read into them is merely a way of protecting oneself—very poorly, we might add—against drives of which one prefers to remain altogether ignorant. Is it, in the end, conceivable that the little girl who wants to sleep with her father[10] could express herself in such a manner if she has received no signals from her father that allow her to create these phantasms? Phantasms are not imaginary productions that come out of nowhere. In this case, they have been inscribed in the little girl's body by the father himself. The opposite phenomenon can be seen in people who seem to be forbidden to have phantasms and dreams: they are that way because, as children, they lacked the incestuous loves and desires that would normally have surrounded them. The fact that parents don't want to hear anything about this—and psychoanalysts don't either[11]—doesn't make the slightest difference. In those for whom incest has never been thinkable or possible, one sees an absence of subjectivity, the abolition of the possibility for differences, and along with it the transformation of the individual into a machine who can only realize his destiny through another.

This mundane observation can be transposed to the psychoanalytic cure. When Freud tells us that psychoanalysis is a cure accomplished through love, he is obviously thinking of the patient's love for the analyst. There can be no question of the analyst's love for the patient. That is prohibited, that is dangerous. The analyst is only a mirror, a receptor. And transference, or the invention of transference as an operative concept, must remain at that level. But this conception is false. How could a given trait of the analyst—the color of his eyes, the tone of his voice, the curve of his nose, a glimpse of his hand—how could all of that become the anchor point for incestuous desires if the analyst himself did not seek to seduce, was not in love in some manner, and was not filled with incestuous desires (and not by the Desire for Desire with capital *D*s)? It is silly to refuse to recognize this. As if a patient could possibly be cured of the morbid pleasure that provides all neurotic and psychotic mechanisms with what they need to renew themselves, to shift in direction, and to invent new faces for themselves, unless the analyst had at his disposal a force of equal vigor, density, and speed!

This point should be taken even further. If the realization of these incestuous desires is not really possible, they are nothing. They only exist if they tend toward satisfaction. Many people have confused two things that are utterly distinct: the prohibition on incest and the impossibility of incest. A friend of mine who is neither stupid nor uneducated, to whom I said the other day that I was getting ready to write something about incest, broke in: "You mean to say, the incest prohibition." It would thus seem that one can no longer speak of incest in any context other than that of prohibition, which blurs its existence and value on the one hand and its possibility on the other. However, the prohibition on incest changes nothing about its real possibility. There would be no prohibition, least of all one that is constantly repeated, if incest were purely and simply impossible. Certain anthropologists are less hurried to deny the existence of incest. As Lévi-Strauss put it, "Incest is fine, as long as it's kept in the family."[12] This is a way of saying that incest does quite well as long as society doesn't intervene to interrupt it; but it is also a way of recognizing implicitly that incest must play its role at the heart of the family so that society, through an operation of derivation, can function. The incest prohibition is usually said to be necessary to prevent society from dying, but no one recalls that the same thing would happen if incest were not practiced. The primary force is that of incest; the prohibition that diverts this force onto other objects cannot produce it, but merely make use of it. Everyone knows this, and anthropologists maintain that the only goal of exogamy is to carry out, through a detour, a more or less obvious endogamy. Nor does this escape the notice of psychoanalysts: marriages or sexual unions reproduce, positively or negatively, model bonds to a father, mother, brother, or sister. In a word, the realization of incest is not only possible but necessary, even if it is through an intermediary; without it, every form of relationship among human beings would become exhausted.

The crucial question is that of the detour, for in matters of incest, we are always in the realm of the "too much" or "not enough." And it is here, no doubt, that we should look for one of the reasons for the radical instability of individual consciousness. When incestuous desire is at work, how can it be deployed to the proper degree? If this desire entails the most forbidden primary violence, it can only be denied or drive the person mad. The child who speaks during psychoanalysis will always complain about a lack or an excess of affection and caresses. When Freud said that in matters of education one is always a loser, he may have had this in mind. That psychoanalyst who asserts that children should not be kissed must be thinking of the excesses of physical contacts that give rise to psychotics; but we can also suppose that she herself fears maternal invasions, those to which she was subjected or those that she inflicted. Psychotics who are lacking in a human individuality (or who are a caricature of that quality) can be found just as readily among those whose bodies were not pampered and who cannot as a result appropriate their own history for themselves.

Moreover, the "too much" and "not enough" can be switched around so as to produce identical results. Is it the incestuous mother, or the frigid mother, who forbids her son from having any woman or sends him on an indefinite quest to have all women, so that he never attaches himself to any woman and so that she, the mother, remains unique?[13] Is it the incestuous father, or the father who is incapable of desiring his daugher, who makes her a virgin for no man or a prostitute for anyone at all? To answer those questions we would have to be able to go back to a mythic time before the incest prohibition—that is, to be able to decide which part of the desire for incest arises from the incestuous object and which part arises from its prohibition. The faces of desire are, in our era, indissociable, and that is why the greatest force can always take the appearance of the least. The separation that is necessary for the individual, combined with the bond that is no less necessary, can only operate through a fragile intertwining of the "too much" and "not enough."

A similar problem is raised in the psychoanalytic cure. If the psychoanalyst gives free rein to his desire and to the seduction, he creates an indissoluble bond that might give the analysand the illusion of living, but that in reality binds his patient and prevents him from having any other life; if he is indifferent and lacking in desire toward his patient, nothing happens even after years of so-called analysis. But the difficulty lies in the fact that the incestuous desire is not perceived by the parties involved any more than it is between parents and children; they only become aware of it after the fact. However much the psychoanalyst may try to protect himself through counterphobic behavior, silence, temperate speech, or coldness, the desire or absence of desire passes from one person to the other through a look, an intonation, or the slightest gesture. Let us suppose that a psychoanalyst who is utterly convinced by what he has read here takes as a criterion for accepting or refusing to undertake analysis with someone the possibility or impossibility of having sexual relations with him or her. He cannot, however, form such a hypothesis because he cannot make that judgment; what passes between him and the analysand is unconscious. Parents never know either what aspect of the founding incestuous desire they pass on to a given child, even if they claim to know; they may read all the psychology books and adopt the most carefully chosen attitudes, but there will always be something else, something essential and unsuspected, that passes between them and their children and that will be decisive for the latter. Reductive behaviors may hide an absence of desire whereas a superficial indifference may, on the contrary, allow an overly violent desire to show through by secret pathways. There are rocks that are burning hot and suns that turn objects to ice. The analyst who is engaged in a cure encounters an essential difficulty here: he finds it impossible to handle as he wishes the thing that is the very mainspring of analysis, and impossible to know at the outset what his own degree of investment will be, even though everything will depend on it.

However, this inability to predict whether the mainspring of analysis will or will not work in a given case (the inability to predict is an impossibility to control, and thus to direct) stems from the very essence of that mainspring. To be effective, desire supposes the failure of control. Is there any seduction, any amorous state, any passion (and, thus, any transference) that is not immersed in uncertainty over the nature and effects of one's relationship to the other person? Is that relationship a chain or a passport, a hindrance or freedom? Is love going to be life-giving, or will it change into a mortal hate? Without these uncertainties nothing could ever come into play, because, without them, there would be no risk; and without risk, there would never be any chance for novelty and invention, and never any desire that is put at stake and thus already lost. Psychoanalysts cannot continue to say that they have nothing to do with this process, or that all of this is pure theatrics. If they say that, it is because they cannot bear not knowing how they are involved except after the fact and partially. Seduction, and thus love, and thus transference, function not on the basis of a satisfying object or an object to be satisfied, nor of a lack that is supposedly represented by silence or retreat; rather, they operate on the basis of an undecidable factor: Am I going to become the plaything or the automaton of the other person, or will he or she be it for me? Or, on the contrary, will I be, will he or she be, a bit more alive, a bit more distinct, different, free? As long as Nathanaël in Hoffman's tale *The Sandman* loves the strange beauty of Olympia, he believes her to be alive; the confirmation that she is a doll drives him mad.

The anguish of *Unheimlich*, or the familiarly strange, is at the very heart of the existence of the human individual. The thing that is closest to him is also what escapes him and scares him the most. He is doomed to return to it constantly, only to try to escape from it once more. And that is undoubtedly why incest, the desire for incest, and the prohibition on incest constitute a paradigm of this situation. How can one create distance with this dangerous proximity? Why do the lengthy journeys of exogamy lead us inexorably back to the most obvious endogamy? If the individual was constituted once and for all, if separation was definitively established, if differences never faced collapse, if one knew who is the other and who is one's self, there would be no humanity nor the bittersweet taste of desire either.

Thanks to the conjunction of incest and its prohibition, thanks to the intermingling of the "too much" and the "not enough," thanks to the anguish of the near and the far, the individual is able to constitute himself; but he will always do so through a game that he must constantly relearn and renew. In psychoanalysis, in education, in politics, the dice are thrown on the carpet not once but every day. Incestuous desire is only operative for the individual if it remains really possible; but that possibility, to remain a possibility, must continue to be the effective deviation, the current derivation, of incest. If the incest is forgotten, misunderstood, repressed, or challenged, the individual will be trapped within the internal prison of abandonment or mortal depression. If the incest is directly practiced, and the individual only has eyes, ears, and genitals for his closest relations or their representatives, he will always be on the verge of division and dissolution. All of these hypotheses remain available to everyone, and everyone uses them according to his history and circumstances. But no one ever finishes the process of awkwardly combining these diverse parameters.

*   *   *

The hypothesis according to which the incest prohibition is the operator that makes it possible to produce difference, under circumstances in which the identical threatens to impede the functioning of a particular culture, is seductive[14]; however, it may not account for all the aspects of the question. Another tendency comes to light in numerous civilizations. These civilizations draw from the incest prohibition extreme consequences that bring everything back to the identical. The separation of the political individual is no longer uncertain, but it has undoubtedly been accomplished at the price of losing differences that are no longer set into play in relation to the risk of the identical. From the Greeks, who believed that women were not really part of the human race (only the *aner* is *anthropos*),[15] to the Amazon Indians, who aim for "absolute endogamy" by referring solely to paternal lineage,[16] to many other peoples for whom the incest prohibition ultimately serves to protect masculine homosexuality,[17] culture seems able to establish itself only by forgetting the thing that creates nature, sexual reproduction: women are rejected, incest with the mother goes on undetected, and the differences of the sexes is repressed. Shouldn't we consider this distancing of incest as one of the factors that make civilizations mortal? Like an individual, a society that turns its back on the sources of desire can only become more and more anemic, more and more fragile. Having forgotten where its strength lay, it can only subsist through constraint and give political subjects a purely abstract identity while forbidding them to multiply differences.

Perhaps our civilization is going to go even further into abstraction. The technical object is constantly exerting more and more domination over the economic and political.[18] The dream or nightmare of our era is not just that individuals are becoming interchangeable and man is being replaced by machines, but that life is being fabricated and living beings turned into automatons. Everything that is invented, particularly around processes of reproduction and gestation, is merely the most spectacular aspect of an attempt to wrest from nature the limit she sets for us and to wrest from desire its risks and its chronic uncertainties. This is no less than an attempt to get rid of the human element that constantly disrupts calculations. It is useless to indulge in nostalgia for the good old days or to denounce scientific progress. But we must surely recognize that, in this environment, the political individual today seems to have at his disposal nothing but two correlative brands of madness: the madness of the paranoid, a subject who is certain of his difference and masterfully maneuvers the universe; and the madness of the subject who has disappeared into the masses, where he hopes to find once more the life of which he has been deprived by forces on every side.[19] Is there still hope that the living body might revolt against technology's implacable attempt to turn it into a machine?

In such a context, psychoanalysis probably owes its success to the fact that, in a modernized form, it is one of the very rare places where sex, relationships of desire, and subjectivity are lived, relived, worked through, and, in a way, put into practice. From this perspective psychoanalysis is not dead, as certain people think or wish it to be. But it is nonetheless pervaded today by two contradictory temptations. One is the temptation to retreat into its own territory, psychic reality, to which therapy supposedly introduces those who undertake it; the risk of this is that psychoanalysis will come to be sufficient unto itself and turn into the marginalized domain of a small set of initiates. The second is to conquer culture by dressing up Freud's discovery with elements borrowed from philosophy, linguistics, or mathematics, thus creating the impression that psychoanalysis is the radical truth which gives meaning to all of those disciplines. The individual who allows himself to give in to those temptations will undoubtedly see several of his uncertainties dim, but, in the process, he will probably lose what he had been looking for: a bit more indeterminable and precarious difference in a world that works relentlessly to suck everything up into the identical.

Chapter 3

The Effectiveness of Psychoanalysis

Where does the effectiveness of psychoanalysis lie? The question is basic and, like all basic questions, it is undoubtedly insolvable. All the more so because it points to an even more basic question: What is the aim of psychoanalysis? That is, what is its goal, what does it seek, what is someone who begins analysis asking for, and what does psychoanalysis think it can provide over the course of the treatment? Put in such terms, these questions open the door to a flood of other questions. Certain people, in fact, would prefer not to speak about treatment, except with infinite caution. Saying, for example, that psychoanalysis aims to cure immediately provokes a veritable hue and cry on the part of numerous psychoanalysts. Psychoanalysis, according to such analysts, is not a psychic treatment, but rather resembles an initiation into the discovery of unconscious processes: it is the means of entry into another world that has its own laws, its masters or wise men, its followers, its believers, and its infidels. One is thus obliged to choose, somewhat arbitrarily, the perspective that one prefers and that one intends to uphold thereafter.

I opt deliberately in favor of psychoanalysis as a course of treatment that aims to produce a cure. But these are words that one must, in turn, define in order to be able to use them as a departure point. I contend that psychoanalysis starts with the presentation of symptoms as the patient feels them: anguish, impotence, relational difficulties, incapacities at work, and so on. It is these symptoms that the psychoanalyst endeavors to relieve, but the method used will not be direct, as it might be in medicine; one cannot and must not limit oneself to them, but rather use long detours that will eventually make it possible to reach the desired end. Let us use a comparison: if a radio is broken, there is no point in examining it at length in that state; instead, one should (for example) check each of the transistors one by one and repair them. Likewise, it is not the least bit helpful to listen indefinitely to the complaint that arises from a patient's symptoms; rather, if I can put it in these terms, one should review the psychic circuits one by one and make them function again. Given that it is the entire machine that is engorged, or shrunken, or stiffened, one must undertake to restore its life by making life circulate in it again.

This mechanical comparison is awkward and perhaps offensive, but it simply underscores that a cure, defined by Freud in a felicitous little formula as the possibility of increased activity and enjoyment, can only be obtained through long detours.

These various declarations should suffice to allow me to advance the thesis that I will defend in this essay: there can be a cure, in this sense, because *over the course of analysis, a force is transmitted that tends to produce difference.* These are terms that may account for the effectiveness of psychoanalysis, if I succeed in giving them substance. In the process, we may see that psychoanalyzing has a certain relation to educating and governing—verbs that, according to Freud, represent the three impossible professions.

Let us begin with the fundamental rule that defines the characteristic method of psychoanalysis: to say everything, even the things that seem useless, nonsensical, or disgraceful. In everyday life, speech is supposedly designed to communicate and to transmit information, but also, obviously, to avoid transmitting information. Underlying the use of language are more or less explicit intentions and a wish to express something or to keep it silent. The fundamental rule of psychoanalysis proposes a radically different use of language. Here, it is a question of trying to speak without intention and to let words come out anyway at all, without concern for any syntax whatsoever—that is, independently of an organization imposed by a conscious will. This is an apprenticeship in a language that opens toward other, intentionally unforeseen meanings, toward other reasons, other aims; it entails letting language become diffracted, in a way that not only produces multiple meanings but also leads to meanings that would be intolerable for the self-image that one had or that one wanted to give to oneself or others. It means practicing systematically what I propose calling "un-speech" [*déparole*]. (I have created this neologism to underscore that the speech uttered in psychoanalysis is radically different from what is usually meant by the term.) Un-speech is similar to delirium, in that it is speech that has been undone, a drifting speech that is no longer concerned with being directed at someone or inscribed in a social relationship in anticipation of an action or plan. It is also similar to slips of the tongue, because it tends to express what one wanted to hide, what one wanted to say neither to other people nor to oneself. It is a kind of speech that escapes the speaker. All of that is sufficiently well known that we do not need to dwell on it further.

We should, however, determine under what condition un-speech is possible. For it is not only unusual, it is also dangerous. If the patient hesitates to engage in it, it is because he associates it with the threat of desubjectivization, the loss of elementary control over his own statements. He may find himself invaded by something he had not foreseen, something that will make him abandon the points of reference to which he is accustomed to referring in order to conduct his existence and maintain the minimal self-image that assures him continuity. It is an unknown other that appears before him and in which he no longer recognizes himself. To embark on such an adventure, he must have sufficient confidence in the analyst, who may know how to slow down or stop the un-speech when it threatens to submerge the person who is speaking it. If the un-speech does not become delirium it is because, unlike delirium, it is in fact directed at another person who is supposed to hear it, a person who is, in a sense, the subject of the un-speech but who is not destroyed by it because of that. The psychoanalyst must be an other who does not care about the social consequences of the words exchanged, and who does not have intentions or wishes that are tied to the accomplishment of certain goals.

However, the psychoanalyst is not nothing: he cannot be devoid of any desire, intention, or aim, or he would become a being out of a dream or a phantom. To keep un-speech from becoming delirium, he can turn himself into a protector; but, in order for this un-speech actually to take place—that is, for socialized language to be undone—one must suppose the presence of a singular force that tears apart the intra-social fabric. What is that force? Freud sometimes describes the analysand's transference onto the analyst by using the words "confident" or trustful expectation (*glaübige Erwartung*). The patient expects the analyst to provide the solution of his difficulties and relief from his suffering, and the confidence he invests in the analyst enables him to abandon his ordinary way of speaking, because he has put himself into a state of suggestibility and because the bond he has created with the analyst makes the values or interests proposed in the social field ridiculous and worthless. This confident expectation can, however, describe the analyst's position just as well. Indeed, it is the analyst's confident expectation that underlies the possibility of un-speech on the part of the analysand.

The psychoanalyst expects. He does not suggest anything. He doesn't propose any task other than that of allowing any kind of speech to come to the fore. One could say that he is expecting un-speech. However, if he were expecting nothing but that, it would never come. In reality, he is expecting the forces—in Freudian language one might say, perhaps, the repressed forces or drives—that will be able to undo social language, to shatter it, to create a breach in the protective glacis that forbids those forces to appear, lest they compromise civilized life. In other words, the analyst is expecting the patient to emerge from his tomb and awaken, and he expects nothing but that, at bottom. This expectation may, however, be nothing more than that of the curious onlooker enjoying the spectacle of the raging sea that smashes whatever its waves encounter. If that was the only ingredient of the analyst's expectation (even if it might come into play in such a form over the course of an analysis), it is likely that nothing would happen, because the analysand's fear would be accentuated in the process, and he would retreat into a careful silence or create a diversion through words that had no significance for him.

One can, first of all, describe this expectation in the most banal terms: the analyst trusts the analysand, but in a way that differs from the analysand's trust for him. While the analysand expects the analyst to get him out of his predicament, the analyst expects the analysand to get *himself* out of his predicament. The analyst places his trust in the analysand: he hypothesizes that the analysand will sort things out, he believes it and has faith in him. It is *this sort of expectation* and confidence, this belief, that is effective and that constitutes, in and of itself, a *transmission of force*. This is a very common experience: one need only listen to someone or take an interest in his statements for him to say far more than he would to anyone, and for him not to fear exposing himself through his words.

Psychoanalysis may do nothing more than isolate this experience and systematize it. Listening gives the other person the strength to speak, and listening in a state of indecision over the goals of the exchange gives the strength of un-speech. Indecisiveness means that any kind of speech is possible and that no particular kind is sought. The force transmitted by the expectation is the force that opens a space of possibilities for a condition that seems irremediable—namely, the situation of a suffering patient.

(We have undoubtedly identified the first and last driving force underlying education, and perhaps even teaching. The destiny of the children whose parents have trusted and believed in them is utterly different from that of other children. It is widely recognized that a professor who knows how to inspire confidence can make the most recalcitrant students succeed in his discipline. The obvious difference between education and psychoanalysis is that the latter does not use the mediation of any task; it thus shows the relationship of expectation for what it is, which has a whole series of consequences. It is, however, a safe bet—a gratuitous bet, given that it is unverifiable—that there would be far less need to resort to school psychologists or child psychoanalysts if teachers did not transmit generalized doubt and depression. But that depends, of course, on a whole series of networks that are peculiar to society.)

Psychoanalysis isolates, therefore, in order to turn that isolation into the driving force behind an artificial experience, a driving force that is present in every properly human elaboration—in every development of humanity, if you will. Let us try to delve further into the description of this phenomenon. The indecisiveness of the expectation that produces un-speech can be considered an act of violence. It is a disruption that terminates the plans and tasks that had occupied the analysand's attention and creates a suspense that unmasks the primitive forces that are usually channeled and modified by intentional thought and action. Initially, therefore, indecisiveness creates a chaos and disorder that may become the opportunity for liberating these forces and thereby reviving the psychic life of the patient. To do so, however, this indecisive expectation must combine with the effect that is intended (and thus determined) by that expectation: namely, the provocation of the other person into a state of alterity and distinction.

It is widely acknowledged that the patient's expectation is the principle that underlies suggestibility—that is, his dependence in regard to the analyst. If that were the only factor at play, there would be room for nothing except the patient's progressive absorption into the analyst's conscious or unconscious desire, thoughts, and will. By contrast, because it is indecisive about the form and manner the patient will adopt but decisive in its aim of provoking the patient to produce himself, the analyst's expectation induces the patient to turn his back on dependency and embrace self-determination by setting his distinctive limits. In dependency, a dream of omnipotence is always present, whereas the provocation to self-production represents the abandonment of that dream in favor of the process of partialization and relativization—in other words, the process of differentiation.

The analyst's expectation can also be described as the opening of a space of possibilities. It refuses, in fact, to consider the patient's current situation as definitive or ineluctable, and it hypothesizes that things can be modified, that there is room for a new history. Obviously, this expectation must be precise, and it must be well founded, too. An overly broad expectation that was not based on what is truly possible, on real grounds for expectation, would be no more than a fiction that could not permit any change to occur. On the other hand, an expectation that was too narrow or too limited in its ambitions would not suffice to trigger the adventure of un-speech and its possible beneficial consequences. In a sense, the psychoanalyst, after the fashion of the government leader, must be a visionary. Clearly, unlike the politician, he doesn't have to propose a grand scheme that is punctuated with projects to fulfill, yet he must already sense and foresee the multiplicity of possibilities that the patient can achieve. Psychoanalysis is often interpreted as a process that raises up the buried past ("The hysteric suffers from reminiscences"); as such, it fails to understand that the thing that gives access to the constitution of a past is the chance for a future. If it is not already tomorrow, then it is not yet yesterday. What supports tomorrow is expectation. If psychoanalysis, like education and politics, is an impossible profession that is because it must, contrary to all expectations, trace the path toward what is possible, regardless of the insurmountable facts.

The best way of characterizing the analyst might be through the term "passion for alterity," if we can venture to call it that. This passion should not be confused with altruism and its devotion, nor with the kind of love that intends to last and is secretly founded on a reciprocal interpenetration. Instead, this passion is the necessary condition for the other to exist, for differentiation to be enacted, and for separation and distinction to be carried out. That, moreover, is why this passion can be no more than a technique (as opposed to a mode of life) that contains its own temporal limit in that it is only practiced through the discontinuity of moments, and its internal qualitative limit in that it is only practiced under the artificial circumstances of a situation that is abstracted from ordinary existence. This is a special type of passion, in the sense that it is constantly in mourning for itself, because the passion of passion is to maintain its object at all cost. This passion is thus fundamentally ambiguous, not only because it is infinitesimally close to what is at the origin of hypnotic fascination, but also because in the analyst it takes root in its opposite: namely, his undying doubt over his own identity and difference. The passion for alterity constantly feeds upon the threat of the collapse of all alterity: it develops on the basis of the fear of a dissolution and a loss of limits. Wanting an other, even if that other were to become the most fearsome adversary, may not stem from an excess of overflowing forces or an overabundant generosity, but rather from the need to have someone, at least one person, get to the place I am not certain to reach.

If transference is described as a confident expectation, or as a process by which the analysand entrusts himself to the analyst, one could well call countertransference the analyst's expectation of the analysand's alterity. Ordinarily, the word *countertransference* designates the sentiments that tie the analyst to his patient and hinder the former's receptivity, or the emotions felt by the analyst and the thoughts they trigger, which must be analyzed in order to avoid blocks in the treatment. But couldn't one say, more radically, that countertransference is the analyst's need for the alterity of the analysand, as we just described it? In that case, we would have to call the passion for alterity *anti-transference*, implying that one didn't need the other person to be free and differentiated (because one was oneself) and as a consequence, that it were possible for the other to become truly separate. But, in reality, what distance is there between countertransference and anti-transference, so defined? One can just as easily answer that the distance is total, or that it is nonexistent. It would be total if the passion for alterity could be developed for itself and be cheerfully and definitively distinguished from the need for the alterity of the other. It is nonexistent if this passion does not come and go and if it cannot temporarily cease needing the other as an other. We are dealing here with a paradox that must be explored further, for although it lies at the heart of psychoanalysis, it is necessarily a founding rule for education and a principle of government as well.

Fabricating another human being, or wanting to fabricate another human being, is a contradictory expression because it initially seems to be able to lead nowhere but to an object that, by definition, will remain an object and never be an other. But fabricating another person also includes the possibility and the risk that this desired birth (or reproduction of one's self) will provide that object with an opportunity to take its distance and operate according to its own laws, like the statue of Pygmalion that was brought to life by Aphrodite. One can suppose that, in every human subject, there is a beginning of independence that has been present from the start. The analyst will strive to play on that precondition, instead of crushing it definitively. A little French girl, in answer to her father's suggestion that she take up English after she had studied so many other subjects, exclaimed: "I'm fed up. I'm not a doll you can teach different things just for fun. I'm alive. I'm alive." Making another person can, therefore, mean producing an automaton, and that is practically always what an educator (or an analyst) cannot avoid having as an aim, whatever customary justifications he may give. There will, however, always be crucial moments when the automaton awakes. The decisive stakes will thus lie in the action the analyst takes in the face of this revolt: he might respond with anger and a more subtle coercion that will force the recalcitrant to return to the state of a docile object, or he might respond with astonishment, creating the sort of moment when the choice of the other is validated by a retreat. It is as if the analyst says: "This revolt belongs to him, so I will let him appropriate it: I will abandon the ambiguity of my approach in this instance and allow him to get away from me, for I am dealing with the strange event of a patient making the slight but infinite passage from the state of an automaton to that of a living being."

The passage from countertransference to anti-transference (which is the only thing that permits the dissolution of transference to occur) is thus conditioned by the analyst's reaction to the initial effects of the passion for alterity. In other words, it is a question of knowing whether this passion, when it has obtained what it was seeking—namely, the other—will repudiate itself by re-ducing alterity to nothing, or whether it will instead suspend itself in order to be completely carried out. The analyst will therefore go from countertransference to anti-transference if the passion for alterity can be interrupted, or if it ceases, either in relation to the patient, who is given the space he demands, or on its own terms—that is, if the analyst renounces the need for the other because he has stopped doubting that there is a minimal difference between them. A temporal limit that is set on this passion through its sus-pension, and an internal limit that is set through the certainty of an identity that is reflected back by the other—these are the con-ditions of possibility for anti-transference. For the psychoanalyst who is pursuing his experiment, the risk of losing his sense of self is always present in that he is more and more aware of the personal need that underlies his professional efforts to create difference be-tween himself and his patient; but, on the other hand, the need for an other becomes less and less pressing because the analyst realizes that the repetition of his professional function provides no remedy for his own problem, and that he is primarily concerned with the improbability that the other will be brought into being as a different human being. It is thus this improbability that he must confront and work through.

Freud constantly associated the effectiveness of analysis with the act of becoming aware of unconscious desires—in other words, with the lifting of repression and the passage of certain desires from the unconscious to consciousness. But these aftereffects of the ideology of the Enlightenment were then replaced by an occasional return to the necessity of abreaction, according to the method learned from Breuer—that is, the acting out of that which could not be done during childhood. It is in this second perspec-tive that the work of analysis must, I think, situate itself today, because the loss of identity or the absence of identity is the cen-tral illness from which our civilization is suffering and because this identity has to be made, constructed, against the threat of chaos and dissolution. Only the expectation of the analyst (or of the edu-cator or government leader) can aim for that identity, desire it, wish for it, and thus give it the force it needs to come into being. Let us underscore once again that this force is transmitted if, and only if, it is outlined in the analyst against the constitutive weak-ness of his own identity. Psychoanalysis brings to light this question, this illness, and the possibility of a solution, because it makes that force operate in its crudest form, unobscured by the mediation of a subject matter or a technique or a behavior that must be learned, or through the necessity of tasks to be accomplished.

It is useful, at this juncture, to retrace our steps. We have posited that the analyst's confident expectation regarding the analysand is necessary to remove the danger and the difficulty of un-speech. But where does this un-speech lead? By undoing socialized speech and destroying the reference points of a language that is directed at someone, it lets certain drives come to light, in all of the disorder of speaking: namely, the primitive interests that civilization seeks to control, to divert, or to proscribe and that can be reduced under the categories of money, sex, and death to theft, rape, and murder. The person engaged in un-speech discovers that he is inhuman: in other words, he discovers that far from tending to establish stable and civilized relations with his fellow creatures, he tries to exploit them to the point of destroying them. How, having made the irrepressible discovery of this inhumanity, might he manage to return to the human?

This regression is doubly unbearable because it signifies the loss of the illusory identity to which the analysand had been accustomed and because the identity that takes its place—that of a thief, a rapist, and a killer—opens the door to an upheaval in his social relations. The reflex, in this instance, is to hold the analyst responsible not for the discovery, but for the situation it creates, and to make him pay for it one way or another—in other words, to enter into conflict with him. Faced with this new vitality, whose roots extend into the depths of the inhuman, and with these forces, whose violence is astonishing and fearsome, the analysand decides that it is time to exercise them—first of all, in regard to the sorcerer's apprentice who unleashed them. Under such circumstances, analysis inevitably becomes a confrontation, and the analyst turns into an adversary. It is probable that the analyst, surprised by attacks that will strike him precisely where he is most vulnerable, will react, with all sorts of good reasons, by shifting more or less onto the territory of the analysand and by becoming a thief, rapist, or killer for him. One could say a good deal more about the necessary passage through this conflict and about the strategies that make it possible to work one's way out of it. But that would take us too far afield. We should simply underscore that, although the analyst cannot avoid accepting the confrontation without which the awakened primitive forces can never develop, he must return to the state of expectation in order to free himself from the conflict. The submerged analysand denies any alterity and will thus try to strike at its principle by making the analyst abandon the position from which he might open up new forms of life in the analysand's existence. It is by maintaining a distance between that inevitable confrontation and the state of expectation that the analyst will enable the patient to postpone the realization of his drives and thus to tame and humanize them once again. The force communicated through the analyst's confident expectation enables the analysand to cross this space where forces surge forth that he cannot control but that, thanks to the analyst who accompanies him in this transformation, he already knows will not carry him away.

However, this regression toward theft, rape, and murder, where human interests are presented in a dehumanized form before being converted and brought back to humanity, is only possible in the most favorable cases. For psychotics, or those who are called "borderline," the situation is different. In a sense, they have never been admitted into human relations. What they have known of the human is the inhuman, the side of humanity that manifests itself in self-absorption and rejection. They were unable to identify with those around them, even at the risk of dying; and, to protect themselves from this inhuman element that formed them, they have had to take refuge in the infra-human realm or in the not-yet-human realm of animals, vegetables, and minerals (which is nonetheless a condition of the human). They are bodies of stone that can neither suffer nor enjoy, because something that has been reduced to the state of an object is forbidden to suffer and because enjoyment is not the business of an individual who has been deprived of all interiority. They are like plants that are incapable of locomotion, because it is impossible for them to detach themselves from the site where they are placed; they must consequently stay where they are, attached, and unable to know absence, which would be fatal for them. Although they are sometimes dangerous animals, their dangerousness is rooted in unconsciousness and a pure spontaneity that knows nothing of the succession of time and what it can modify; they are, as a result, caught in the pure repetition of the same tedious instant.

In analysis, therefore, they will have to be able to repeat the passage through this nonhuman element that constitutes them. The psychoanalyst's expectation will recognize them as already human in these states, which were necessary for their survival and in which they protected themselves, in their madness, from relationships that were devoid of all humanity. It is easy to hear them because they are witnesses to a forgotten history that no one can neglect adopting as his own if he wants to have a chance of reaching the human state. Our history does not consist merely of events tied to people. And the idea that our childhood was made purely out of hatred for our father and love for our mother (or vice versa—and let us not forget the nanny) is greatly impoverished. The little girl needed a doll, but also stuffed animals, for she played with cats as if she were one of them. If children, even in cities, are so eager to have pets around, it is undoubtedly because they need them in order to tame their own animality. And consider that little boy, threatened by his parents, who took refuge in a grove of trees in order to recover his courage. His life would have been different if he had had nowhere to hide except a stone wall. The kingdoms that have preceded the human kingdom in evolution, whose existence is resumed within the human being, are thus a part of our past; there is no need to invoke phylogenesis for this to be real, nor to resort to symbolics in order to show the shortcomings of the theory that ascribes a sacrosanct omnipresence to language. We have, through the simple game of identifications, been this rock, that tree, and that dog; thanks to that, we have already been others, already different in our identity.

Regarding the borderline patient, the psychoanalyst's expectation must operate more than ever as an opening onto a future, for this kind of patient prefers to confine himself to the territory of the nonhuman, where he no longer risks being liquidated. For him, every future is marked with the sign of the inhuman—a human world where he is refused admission and where he is unable to find his way because he knows nothing of the laws that govern it. Opening a future for him will, first of all, mean spending hours going over fossils, forests, and beasts, to the point that the psychoanalyst runs the risk of losing himself in the process. It is by running this risk that the analyst will be able to introduce the echo of a human world from which he comes and where he is still situated. For this patient to relearn or learn to awaken from the dormant state of stones, to walk without worrying constantly about his roots, to speak a language that wants to be heard, the psychoanalyst must unlearn the supposed superiority of the world of humans. As for the expectation for the future, it is his own that is at issue. He must retrace the path of his own improbable future; for who knows what is truly human, who knows whether the human is not a fragile fire that must be rekindled every day?

If confident expectation entails on the one hand provoking the primitive forces that are linked to the interests of money, sex, and death and, on the other hand, reintegrating the kingdoms that preceded the appearance of man and on which the human is constantly predicated, then we should perhaps try to locate the effectiveness of psychoanalysis not so much, as Freud thought, in the act of deciphering historical truth—that is, deciphering traumatic events linked to the personal relationships of childhood—but rather, in the redeployment of the inhuman and the reassumption of the nonhuman. In this sense, one can say that psychoanalysis constitutes a history that did not necessarily take place, for never before have these primitive forces been awakened and never before has the contact with the mineral, vegetable, and animal been historicized. The psychoanalytic cure may, therefore, consist not in the reconstitution of a forgotten history, but rather in its production on the basis of that which has never come to light, or of divisive identifying traits.

There remains a question that should be reopened, even if we cannot develop it—a question that all those who have had to deal with psychoanalysis, from near or far, will not fail to ask themselves: what is the place of language in the conception of psychotherapy that has just been sketched here? The first answer is negative: language is to be considered as an obstacle. It is everything that is revealed by the human/inhuman distinction of the established order, accepted values, fixed relationships, and moribund thinking. The un-speech of analysis must break down this protective glacis: it must dislocate it, bore into it, and fill it with holes, so that a new energy can be injected. Disdaining the established language in this way means opening the door to madness, but it also gives the patient the chance to discover his future dignity. For the value of language in analysis—this is the second answer and this one is positive—lies in the act of giving voice to the inhumanity expressed by the violence of money, sex, and death and in giving voice to the nonhumanness of the other kingdoms. The nonsense of un-speech is succeeded by a kind of meaning in which human-ness perceives itself to be a stranger to itself. This is still a defeat, but it is one that conquers buried and forgotten fields where the individual thought he didn't have to recognize himself. It is thus quite true that language is at the heart of analysis, but certainly not as a unique realm from which one should never stray. Language is at the center because it must confront that which is its enemy, that which threatens to dissolve it, and because it owes its salvation solely to the fact that it becomes the servant of what is foreign to it.

Chapter 4

On the Epistemology of Psychoanalysis

> The knowledge of history, in its origins, does not consist in ferreting out primitive lore or a collecting of bones. History is neither half nor whole natural science; if it is anything at all, it is a mythology.
>
> Heidegger, *An Introduction to Metaphysics*

How can we talk about the epistemology of psychoanalysis? First, what does such an epistemology entail? Probably very different things, depending on the individual. It is thus all the more important to explain what we associate with this concept. Epistemology is the science of knowledge. It attempts to answer these questions: How, within a given discipline, does knowledge operate? By what means does knowledge become established within a particular field? What procedures are used by a science or discipline to constitute its object or objects? What degree of certainty is a discipline capable of reaching, given the means at its disposal? What sort of truth does the discipline propose?

When associated with psychoanalysis, the word "epistemology" thus raises questions not only of method, but of object and of validity as well. Those questions are quite daunting for our discipline, given that we have grown so familiar with psychoanalytic knowledge that we regard it as a self-evident truth. We use the vocabulary of Freudian, Kleinian, Bionian, and Lacanian theory without questioning the legitimacy of those usages. We carefully avoid wondering about the foundations of our knowledge. We consider the discourse of Freud if we are Freudians, that of Melanie Klein if we are Kleinians, or that of Lacan if we are Lacanians, to be a discourse that speaks the truth and that we supposedly need only to assimilate, reproduce, and perhaps develop. In a sense, we are constantly turning our backs on epistemology, whose aim is to give a radical critique of our knowledge by criticizing our modes of knowing.

I would like to rethink this question without taking anything for granted. We are not in the field of the exact sciences: that is, psychoanalysis does not operate according to the accumulation of facts, where the latest discovery is supposedly the one from which one should proceed because it is the most advanced and accounts for all of the preceding discoveries. Rethinking this question from square one means calmly asking oneself this: Is there such a thing as knowledge in psychoanalysis? Is something known in this discipline? And, if so, what?

For my point of departure I will take something that psychoanalysts consider an obvious fact—a fact that is, or that they believe to be, indispensable to their practice, technique, and theory: the discovery of the unconscious. This is an obvious fact, but, as you know, obvious facts are sometimes misleading and are always the source of mistakes, because they prevent us from being surprised by them and from examining them critically.

The unconscious was discovered by Freud; this is a given. Yet, if we read Freud, the discoverer himself, we must qualify that affirmation considerably. In his famous 1915 article on the unconscious, Freud states repeatedly that the unconscious is a hypothesis. Following in the footsteps of many others, he maintains that the unconsciousness is a hypothesis needed to account for certain psychic facts that escape consciousness: principally dreams, symptoms, slips of the tongue, and jokes. Freud's reasoning is quite clear: if one wants to explain these facts, which appear in the absences, gaps, flaws, failures, and disturbances of conscious speech, and if one does not want to settle for regarding these phenomena as pure absurdities or pure mysteries, then one must resort to the hypothesis of an unconscious psychism. By doing so, has one proven the existence of the unconscious? Certainly not. All that one has proven is that, if one wants to preserve the principle of universal determinism (i.e., nothing happens without a cause), one must suppose that there is some psychological element that reestablishes a continuity beyond or below the discontinuity experienced by consciousness.

Most of the time, we forget (as Freud himself often did) that the unconscious is a hypothesis. We say it exists, we assume it to be the effective agent of all aberrant processes. And then, since it exists, since it is a fact, we try to make it express itself: we try to know it, to describe it as one describes external facts; we establish the laws of its functioning, we give it a theory, and so on. However, from the strict perspective of epistemology, all of those elaborations are illegitimate.

Why are they illegitimate? Quite simply because, as Habermas very effectively showed in *Knowledge and Human Interests*,[1] those elaborations are based on the practice of tautology. Psychoanalytic theory, and the theory of the unconscious in particular, does nothing but repeat in a different guise the facts that it is supposed to explain. For example, saying that the unconscious always reproduces the same phenomena, or that it is unaware of contradiction and time, is simply a way of restating the traits that characterize symptoms or dreams by attributing them to the unconscious. Thus, when one wants to submit the theory to empirical proof, the verification is assured beforehand, since the theory is simply a translation of the facts. This is tautological because the theoretical instrument always fits in advance the facts from which it is derived.

And yet, some might counter, the discovery of the unconscious really did take place; this discovery has modified our approach to mental illness, psychological processes, the mysteries of invention, and even numerous aspects of culture. I certainly do not deny that. It is possible, however, to understand and interpret the upheavals brought about by psychoanalysis in a way that is totally different from the one we are accustomed to using. I beg the reader's indulgence in explaining this point by way of a detour.

In his book *The Greeks and the Irrational*,[2] E. R. Dodds attempts to explain how the Greeks situated themselves in relation to the things that exceeded their understanding, troubled them, and impelled them to act. To that end, Dodds discreetly translates everything into psychological terms. He shows, for example, that Homeric man considered himself motivated by irrational, unsystematized drives that he attributed to a source outside of himself. Dodds asserts that, according to the relationship that this civilization maintained with dream life, dreams were comparable to the visit of a parent, a revered being, or a god. He cites Plato's *Laws*, where man is depicted as a puppet possessing only a portion of reality. Finally, he contends that the cult of Dionysus freed its followers from the burden of individual guilt through dance and drunken revel. Similar remarks are made concerning madness and inspiration.

What can we glean from these fascinating observations? First of all, that the people of the twentieth century are not the first to wonder at the strange phenomena that undermine the clarity and mastery of their consciousness and reason. Likewise, they are not the first to invent hypotheses to account for these aberrant phenomena. Instead of supposing the existence of a subconscious, the Greeks imagined gods, the return of the dead, the rule of necessity, and many other things as well. Does this reduce Freud's invention to nothing? By no means. Freud's genius consisted in giving a new name to those forces, higher or lower, that turn us into marionettes. But what made Freud successful, above all, was that he gave those forces a name that could be understood and accepted as true and real by a civilization where science and individualism prevail. On the one hand, Freud affirmed the necessity of the unconscious out of his unshakeable loyalty to the principle of determinism; on the other hand, he described the unconscious as monadic because religions had foundered, leaving the individual alone to face his destiny. Lacan did not do anything different when he grafted the unconscious onto language; with the development of linguistics, ethnology, and cybernetics, language has become the only trait by which man is distinguished from other animals.

Just as our only way of understanding ancient civilizations is to reduce to psychological problems their efforts to organize their disordered actions, dreams, and inspirations, so too, and inversely, we must interpret our need to rationalize the irrational as a slightly modified repetition of what has occurred in other cultures. If the gods were, in essence, nothing more than hypotheses imposed upon the ancients to alleviate their sense of alienation from the self, we should not shy away from thinking that the hypothesis of the unconscious, which responds to the same anxieties, is the new, apparently scientific name for the gods of antiquity. The success of Freud (or that of some of his successors) should undoubtedly be ascribed to the fact that they have given us not just one tiny god, but a veritable pantheon from which each of us can pick and choose as we please.

If we return now to the question of knowledge and knowing in psychoanalysis, what do we discover? This knowledge should pertain to the field's principal discovery, the unconscious. However, to speak of the knowledge about the unconsciousness, or knowledge of the unconscious, is simply a methodological absurdity, an epistemological blunder, at least if the preceding analysis is not completely devoid of sense. Is it possible to know a hypothesis? Is is possible to constitute the body of knowledge of a hypothesis? If we say that we are going to try to decipher the unconscious, this presupposes that the unconscious has not only acquired a real existence, but has surreptitiously become a fact. Such a presupposition is strictly inadmissible.

In that same 1915 article on the unconscious, Freud warns us: "Unconscious processes only become cognizable by us under the conditions of dreaming and of neurosis—that is to say, when processes of the higher, Pcs [preconscious] system are set back to an earlier stage by being lowered (by regression). In themselves they cannot be cognized, indeed are even incapable of carrying on their existence" (*S.E.*, 14:187). This statement is clear, but it is nonetheless constantly forgotten by psychoanalysts. The expression "Freud discovered the unconscious" should be erased from our vocabulary once and for all. In reality (and this is not at all the same thing), Freud *invented* the unconscious in order to account for certain facts.

The decision to study the unconscious or its processes, to establish the logic of the unconscious or uncover its stages, is an operation similar to attempting to describe and know the gods. Certain people have even undertaken the task. The fact of the matter remains that one cannot describe or know the processes of the unconscious; one can only imagine them. From an epistemological point of view, the knowledge of the unconscious must, consequently, be reduced to an effort of the imagination. Since the unconscious is a hypothesis, all we can do in respect to it is to develop the hypothesis from itself, to divide it into small units in proportion to the number of problems we encounter, to invent repression, censure, drives, cathexis, and so on. The psychic apparatus that results from this is in no way the product of a description; it is merely a fiction, an imaginary edifice that engenders partial hypotheses in an attempt to give content to the principal hypothesis. This enterprise is seductive—brilliant, even—but it has more in common with the writing of science fiction than with the constitution of a field of knowledge. From an epistemological point of view, this fiction is similar in every aspect to the invention of a theogony. Freud is our Hesiod. We have become so accustomed to using what we mistakenly name Freudian "concepts" that we have no more critical distance from them than the ancient Greeks had from their gods. We give them the consistency of reality when they are only projections of our imagination.

Have you ever traced the meaning of a Freudian term with the help of the book *Vocabulaire de la psychanalyse* by Laplanche and Pontalis?[3] The results are always the same. Each term, through a series of transformations, acquires varied meanings that, in the end, reveal a contradiction. In other words, every term signifies something and its opposite. You may object that this presents no problem, since the entire theory of the unconscious presupposes the coexistence of opposed terms. In that case, the theory of the unconscious would simply be faithful to its object: it would be a tissue of contradictions without the possibility of logical negation. In fact, however, if the terms used by Freud mean both one thing and its opposite, this simply indicates that there is no index or limit to the work of the imagination. I cannot resist pointing out that one finds exactly the same phenomenon in the study of mythologies: their fundamental principle is the *coincidentia oppositorum*. Moreover, as you know, Christian theologians assert the same thing with respect to that other convenient hypothesis: God. All divine attributes, they maintain, can and must be simultaneously affirmed and denied. This amounts to recognizing that we can say nothing of consequence about them, and that we are engaged here in an operation of pure projection.

It is the nature of an unverifiable hypothesis (unverifiable because it is invented to account for irrational facts) to convey a host of contradictions, without permitting us to judge where the hypothesis may be more true. In reality, it is neither true nor false, since it is situated outside the realm of observable facts. In a footnote to his article on "Feminine Sexuality," Freud comments on the disagreement of women psychoanalysts regarding penis envy and concludes: "The use of analysis as a weapon of controversy can clearly lead to no decision" (*S.E.*, 21:230). In other words, everything that is affirmed in psychoanalysis can just as easily be denied, and we have no means of deciding who is right. One might conclude that psychoanalysis is not yet a science but will be one day. However, it is also possible to consider the situation as incurable because it rests upon the hypothetical nature of the unconscious, a hypothesis that was imagined in order to account for incomprehensible facts, which cannot in turn serve to prove the hypothesis.

The use of narrative or discourse to explain the aberrant facts of human existence has a name in the history of civilizations. It is called mythmaking. Freud was aware, at certain moments, that he was proposing what he called speculations, among other things. In *Totem and Taboo*, in *Moses and Monotheism*, with the notion of the death drive in *Beyond the Pleasure Principle*, Freud knows that he is inventing, even though he persists in trying to prove his theses with facts. All psychoanalytic theory, however, depends upon this very particular type of literary invention. The lucubrations of the seventh chapter of the *Interpretation of Dreams* and the construction of the psychic apparatus are considered to be fictions by Freud himself. But he only mentions this in passing. The rest of the time, his methodological precautions disappear. He believes, and makes us believe, in the reality of his fiction. Nevertheless, if we wish to speak correctly of psychoanalytic epistemology, we must recognize that our belief in no way helps to give the fiction a scientific status.

It was, precisely, while speaking of the *Interpretation of Dreams* that Wittgenstein said to one of his students: "Freud remarks on how, after the analysis of it, the dream appears so very logical. And of course it does. You can start with any of the objects on this table — which certainly are not put there through your dream activity — and you could find that they could all be connected in a pattern like that; and the pattern would be logical in the same way." Further on, he remarked: "Freud refers to various ancient myths in these connections, and claims that these researches have now explained how it came about that anybody should think or propound a myth of that sort. Whereas in fact Freud has done something different. He has not given a scientific explanation of ancient myth. What he has done is to propound a new myth. The attractiveness of the suggestion, for instance, that all anxiety is a repetition of the anxiety of the birth trauma, is just the attractiveness of a mythology."[4]

Wittgenstein was not the only one to notice the mythological character of Freud's work. Jean Hyppolite, in his commentary on the *Verneinung* essay that appears at the end of Lacan's *Écrits*, brings up the theme on several occasions: "I see in the genesis I have described here a kind of great myth." "You can sense the import of this myth that recounts the formation of the inside/outside distinction." " 'There is, in the beginning,' Freud seems to say, but in the beginning means nothing more than the mythic 'Once upon a time.' "[5]

This elementary observation—that psychoanalytic theory is a mythology—is systematically ignored in psychoanalytic circles. Psychoanalysts are in exactly the same situation as the adepts of ancient cults who firmly believed in the existence of Dionysus or Apollo and who speculated on their works and gestures. The resemblance is especially striking in Lacanian circles in France, most particularly in Paris. If you take a look at certain journals you will find yourself confronted with the wildest of lucubrations that take Lacanian doctrine as their point of departure. This doctrine is considered to be a true discourse, speaking the truth about the unconscious, describing the fact of the unconscious. After this basic credo one plunges into pseudotheoretical refinements, reminiscent of theological discussions on the sex of angels or byzantine quarrels over words where the relationship to the object is completely forgotten. It is a kind of cancer of the imagination that develops without internal index or external limit. Criticism, in these circumstances, is both impossible and useless: impossible because, in this field, nothing is proven because there is nothing to prove, and useless because one is dealing with believers who all use the same empty language. To every criticism, they reply in essence: This simply proves that you do not believe. Only the goal of treatment, i.e., the cure, might have served as the functional index in the field of analysis. But since psychoanalysis has been carefully detached from the notion of cure, it is now floating unanchored like Rimbaud's drunken boat.

We are therefore faced with an inevitable question: through what kind of intellectual operation did Lacan succeed in leading psychoanalysis down this path? How did he manage to produce a discourse that seems to give ample guarantee of its own rigor and yet leaves no opening for criticism? It is doubtless an ingenious feat deserving closer examination.

Lacan inherited the hypothesis of the unconscious and realized full well that nothing could be derived from it—in other words, it could not be used to ground a thought system and a theoretical construct. It was thus necessary to establish the unconscious as a fact. To do this, Lacan grafted language onto the unconscious, asserting that language was the condition of the unconscious. This is undoubtedly admissible, for if people did not speak, the unconscious would be impossible to imagine. Thus there is an intrinsic link between the unconscious and language. This is the first step.

A second step is taken with the posing of the adage: *the unconscious is structured like a language*. Obviously this adage has never been proven, nor has its perplexing multitude of meanings been put to the test, since the word *like* can be read as any kind of connection, possible or imaginable. But the adage allows for a third step: in order to know the unconscious, it is enough to know language. More precisely, in order to understand unconscious processes, it is enough to study figures of discourse. Hence, for example, the famous passage from condensation to metaphor and from displacement to metonymy.

Lacan thus ingeniously turned the tables. Having started from a hopeless situation, where all we had to ground a body of knowledge was a hypothesis, he made it seem possible for us to know the unconscious as a fact. Those who feel no need to examine Lacan's operation more closely think that it was a success and that Lacanian doctrine is the revelation of the unconscious. That is why Lacanians think that Lacan went much farther than Freud in giving psychoanalysis a solid foundation. It is evident, however, that the operation I have just described is totally illegitimate. Its execution rests upon a series of confusions. Unconscious processes themselves are confused with the hypothetical processes of dreams or neuroses, those hypothetical processes are confused with real ones, and real processes are confused with linguistic forms. Lacanian theory can only be considered a well-founded theory at the price of all those confusions. Genius and intellectual prestidigitation are here united. Only a mind of the highest order could make us believe that he had transformed a hypothesis into a describable fact.

However, having come this far, we cannot avoid noticing a new twist, which Lacan possibly did not foresee. In a very detailed and very respectful article, published in the *Revue philosophique de Louvain* in 1979, Regnier Pirard shows that Lacan's treatment of language "is more apt to mimic the unconscious than to teach us the meaning of speech. But this raises a question: does psychoanalysis consist in mimicking the unconscious or in making it speak? And isn't a mimetic linguistics a superfluous and impotent redundancy? There is only a short step from that redundancy to the complete evacuation of the unconscious. If the unconscious takes over language to the point of becoming equivalent to it, we might as well say that there is no longer, nor was there ever, an unconscious."[6] This implies that the Lacanian operation is untenable. To transform the hypothesis of the unconscious into the linguistic fact of the unconscious amounts to evacuating, along with the hypothesis, the unconscious itself. During the 1970s it was common for Lacanians to label Lacan's discourse the discourse of the unconscious, and Lacan denied having what is called a thought system. It was a Promethean attempt, supposedly successful, to transplant the entire unconscious into a language designed for this purpose. But the absurdity of the effort is obvious. How could speech escape the laws of consciousness? Moreover, if the unconscious is capable of invading consciousness to such an extent, it no longer exists as an unconscious. In other words, the unconscious cannot simultaneously be a hypothesis that explains certain facts and a fact.

Once again, though, a question arises: why did Freud or Lacan have such success? Why have they since become an integral part of our culture? There are certainly numerous possible answers to that question. However, to stick to the perspective that I have adopted for this essay, I will simply answer: Freud and Lacan managed to invent myths that corresponded to the needs of their time. Like the great mythmakers they set up narratives and discourses that pretended to give meaning to irrational facts. All myths aim to fulfill the anxious expectation of the man who finds himself subject to a destiny he cannot control. By inventing the unconscious, Freud accounted for the fact that we are nothing but marionettes made to speak, act, and suffer through processes that are established in our infancy. By asserting that the unconscious is structured like a language, that desire is grounded in lack, and that analysis defines itself as failure, Lacan invited us to turn our generalized disillusion into the basis for a decisive belief—or rather, of an unassailable illusion.

What, then, can be the role of what we call (erroneously perhaps) psychoanalytic theory? Not all psychoanalytic texts should be placed on an equal footing. Freud's case studies, Melanie Klein's writings, and Lacan's first seminars certainly help us in listening to our patients. Here we are dealing with psychoanalysis, because the practice of a cure is at issue. The categories employed, and the hypotheses invoked to organize the patient's statements, remain flexible and complex. We can use them, change them, abandon them, or invent others. They are useful reference points, even though they are unstable, and our practice constantly leads us to expand them or to contradict them so that we may continue to be aware of what is new or singular. What I am describing here is a pragmatic knowledge that can just as easily aid us as hinder us, if we take it for a fully constituted and definitive body of knowledge. Psychoanalytic practice is an art that relies, first and foremost, on transference and its obscurities, and it cannot aspire to any form of scientificity.

This is not the case for the supposedly theoretical texts, which should be classified unequivocally as mythologies. We can take immense pleasure in discovering Freud's subtleties, or in following Lacan through the endless fireworks he displays before our eyes. But we must not be fooled by these exploits and artifices. They do not help us in our practice, they sterilize thought if we accept them as revelations, and they turn psychoanalysts into the faithful adherents of a sect whose obscurantism rivals that of some religions or political ideologies. We must maintain an extremely critical attitude toward these texts—that is, we must dismantle them as we would a myth or the individual mythology of a neurotic.

I would like to make a remark in passing. When we consider the first generation of Freud's disciples, we are confronted with personalities of great stature and considerable originality: Ferenczi, Tausk, Abraham, Theodor Reik, W. Reich, Jung, and Groddeck. After this generation, once a single doctrine began to dominate, only followers were to be found. The same thing was true of Lacan. His first group of students had their own stature. They spoke their own language, and all of them remained close to clinical practice. After that, a dual phenomenon of sterility and psittacism occurred. Because the Lacanian doctrine was imposed as truth, it invaded the entire field of psychoanalytic preoccupations. It destroyed all originality and all invention. The first students saw the myth taking form before their eyes, but in the meantime they made use of their own histories and their own manner of speaking. The second generation arrived just as the telling of the myth was completed. Partly out of fascination, and partly out of laziness, that generation accepted the myth without asking any questions. This is all the more true when the utterly faithful are there to terrorize those who do not conform meekly to the doctrine. The sect is then fully functioning and it manages to pass off its myths as obvious facts.

Up to now, we have tried to take nothing for granted and to apply the elementary rules of an epistemological critique. In so doing we have been forced to recognize that the consistency of psychoanalytic knowledge was the same as that of myths. Was I, perhaps, wrong to proceed in this fashion? Might another way of approaching this question have yielded different results? That is quite possible, and such an objection should not be dismissed a priori. I shall therefore temporarily abandon all epistemological precaution and adopt the thesis that I contested above—the thesis that the unconscious exists—in order to draw out its principal consequences. We will see whether the results of this procedure allow us to grant psychoanalytic knowledge a more solid foundation.

If the unconscious exists, what happens? What happens to psychoanalytic knowledge? First, how are we to conceive of the unconscious? Whatever means we use to envision the unconscious, whether as a receptacle for drives, desires, and phantasms, or as a treasure house of signifiers, we see it as the force that directs and informs our most specific and characteristic words, gestures, and actions. The discovery of the unconscious made consciousness revolve around it, like Copernicus made the earth revolve around the sun. Ever since this discovery, consciousness has been nothing but the stage of apparent movements that find their reality in the unconscious. This is why Freud writes in *The History of the Psychoanalytic Movement* that consciousness resembles a circus clown who tries to convince the audience that everything taking place in the ring is the result of his will and his commands, whereas those effects are in fact governed by the unconscious. To believe that the unconscious exists is thus tantamount to making it the true motor of human life.

Therefore, if the unconscious exists, everything that consciousness tells us will be subject to suspicion. We can affirm, for example, that our acts correspond to our intentions, but we cannot claim that our explicit and conscious intentions correspond to the real motives behind our acts.

In other words, if we believe in the existence of the unconscious, that belief, far from giving us some form of control, spoils everything: it deprives us of all certainty and shakens the foundations of psychoanalytic knowledge. One can always say that this knowledge is grounded partially in resistance, that it was constituted to effect a repression. The only way to gain control from the existence and knowledge of the unconscious is to forget the definition we ourselves gave to the unconscious.

Precisely because we affirm the existence of the unconscious, what we call psychoanalytic theory can never acquire the status of truth. We must consider it as nothing more than a compromise formation whose structure is identical to the compromises Freud mentions when discussing symptoms and dreams. This theory must, therefore, be analyzed as one would analyze the manifest content of a dream or the characteristics of a symptom.

If, then, we believe in the existence of the unconscious as a fact, we have advanced no further toward founding an understanding of the unconscious, because all knowledge becomes suspect. If the unconscious is a hypothesis, we cannot use it to ground a knowledge of the unconscious. If the unconscious is established as a fact, all knowledge is doubtful.

There is, however, a difference between the two positions: the first leaves open the possibility of striving for rigor whereas the second permanently weakens what we call rigor, logic, or reason. It destroys all the efforts of the intellect and only leaves room for confusion and arbitrariness. I could speak at length about that subject, but I would like to end with a remark that anticipates an objection that some readers will undoubtedly make.

You will probably say or think that I have placed myself outside of psychoanalysis and adopted the point of view of a philosopher. If you are less courteous, you might even say (openly or to yourself) that it is quite clear that I am not a psychoanalyst.

However, if we suppose—purely hypothetically—that I am a psychoanalyst, would it be illegitimate for me to wonder what I am doing? Would it be illegitimate for me to wonder what is the status of analytical theory or to adopt the point of view of reason, or at least of logical rigor, in order to answer that question? Is it scandalous for a psychoanalyst to adopt such a point of view?

I will respond briefly but unhesitatingly to that objection with two arguments. First, Freud never abandoned this point of view. One can even say that his entire endeavor was to rescue a part of human existence from the irrational in order to give the irrational a meaning, a reason, and to reintroduce it into the world of the rational. If Freud shook up a good many certainties and a good many beliefs, he certainly did not do it so that the psycho-analysts who came after him could carelessly return to old beliefs and a denser brand of obscurantism. One could, however, say that something like that is indeed happening today. Psychoanalysts are, moreover, encouraged to take that path by so-called philosophers who are happy to prattle on about certain texts by Freud, and whose most current mode of thinking is nothing more than free association, now dubbed "shift in meaning," "drifting," or "dissemi-nation."

You may tell me that Lacan changed everything. That is obvi-ously false, given that Lacan never stopped striving to derive the logic of the unconscious. It matters little, for my purposes, whether he succeeded or failed. I will simply point out that he never stopped aspiring to the search for truth and its criteria, if only through his attempt to describe the psychoanalytic experience in mathematical terms. It would thus be inappropriate for anyone to try to rely on Freud or Lacan in order to spare himself the worries and pains of intellectual rigor.

I am aware—and this is my last comment—that I have only just begun a project of clarification that will have to be pursued with determination, if only to provide analytical practice with the breathing room it so urgently needs.

Chapter 5

The Laboratory of Cruelty

If we want to speak accurately about an ethics of psychoanalysis, we must ask ourselves what we mean by ethics and by psychoanalysis. The answer is not obvious in either case. Why, for example, should we use the word *ethics* when dictionaries do not really distinguish it from the expression *moral doctrine*? Even if by virtue of some prestigious uses to which it has been put in philosophy the word *ethics* has come to acquire the lofty meaning of the principles suitable for grounding the rules that govern moral behavior, it is, even at that level, merely the Greek transposition of what a moral doctrine worthy of the name can accomplish.

The fact nonetheless remains that the word *ethics* is currently favored by the intelligentsia. These intellectuals undoubtedly wish to avoid the discredit that looms over all moral doctrines, which are by definition moralistic, sanctimonious, and sad and rigid as a result. Speaking of ethics would place us above the rules of a moral doctrine tied to the values and ideals of a particular social group, allowing us to reach the universal character that is involved in all human relations and that determines what makes a relationship between people properly human. Ethics would thus signify the moral code of relationships, or the code that defines the relational rules for all human coexistence. Yet don't all moral doctrines, whether new or ancient, aim to reveal, at last, the operational laws relative to the essence of humanity? It seems, therefore, that we need not distinguish between ethics and moral doctrine. First, that distinction is untenable from the point of view of philosophical tradition; second, when we define ethics in terms of respect for life, concern for truth, recognition of the other, and so on, we necessarily invoke the values that a given group, situated in a particular time and place, considers morally good. To avoid any confusion and any rash claims, it is thus preferable to put the question of the ethics of psychoanalysis in this form: is there a moral doctrine of psychoanalysis?

The question then splits into two: First, do normative rules direct the practice of psychoanalysis? And second, can psychoanalysis become the basis of a new moral doctrine? Those two questions are radically different. The first aims to situate psychoanalysis in relation to a moral doctrine that exists independently of it; this amounts to wondering whether one could formulate a deontology for psychoanalysis—that is, a moral code or set of duties that its practitioners should obey. The second question, which asks whether a moral doctrine can be based on psychoanalysis, involves an ambitious project that should lead to the establishment of specific relationships between humans by virtue of this particular practice.

To know whether a moral doctrine should or can be imposed on psychoanalysis, we must ask ourselves what we mean by psychoanalysis. But we must first remember that every moral doctrine, by dictating the rules that should guide moral behavior and distinguishing good behavior from bad, is concerned with the rights and duties that should govern the establishment and proper functioning of relations between the individuals or groups within a society.

In other words, a moral doctrine strives to maintain the cohesion of a society by specifying the minimal relational norms that are necessary for effective coexistence.

Now, what does psychoanalysis propose? Whatever definition we may give to this discipline, we are obliged to place the fact of transference at its heart. Transference is what Freud very early in his career called a false relationship, since the analysand does not address a real person during the cure, but instead addresses the Other of his dreams, his fantasies, his imaginings. The analyst is obviously not someone who is to be respected, considered, or recognized for what he is. Either he is endowed with disproportionate dimensions, taking on the traits of a fearsome power or of a savior, or he is flagrantly manipulated, forced to wear all of the masks that the analysand wishes to give him. In this case, it is hard to see how normative rules—that is, a moral doctrine of any kind—could be decreed for speech acts that have nothing to do with social reality. What happens in analysis belongs to the most private of private matters, where no social authority applies.

In fact, the psychoanalytic cure is quite often the place where established values are put into question or rejected. It becomes clear, in certain cases, that the rigidity of moral codes passed on by parental figures is one of the reasons for neurosis. Under the pressure of the patient's desires for life and truth these protective scaffolds weaken. Moral doctrine then reveals one of its aspects: it is a set of laws designed to protect individuals from themselves— that is, from the violence and aggressiveness that would provoke violence and aggressiveness in other people, thus creating the infernal cycle of vengeance and reprisals. The goal of moral doctrine is to make coexistence possible among human beings, either by upholding reason—sometimes to the point of smothering animality, all that relates to the instincts and drives, and thus life itself—or by disguising aggressive affects as altruistic sentiments. What psychoanalytic "un-speech" should produce is a suspension of those processes of smothering and disguising. By itself, therefore, un-speech leads to the jungle—that is, to no value beyond that of savagery.

There are even more fearsome and mysterious things at play in analysis that remove us from the realm of moral doctrine. The phenomenon of transference not only produces, for the benefit of an imaginary alterity, an absence of any real alterity; it also prompts the destruction of all alterity in the form of a complacency in morbid suffering. The psychoanalyst naively believes that the analysand who comes to see him in order to express his suffering will do everything possible to be freed from it. That is quite fundamentally not what happens. Thanks to the dependency on the analyst that transference makes possible, the analysand settles into a primitive game of absorption and rejection, fusion and separation, in which he is destroyed as an individuated subject but exalted as a being who is experiencing limitless suffering and passion. The analyst then becomes merely the unwitting instrument of a fixed and repeated destiny. Symptoms appear in this context as the epiphenomenon of that inveterate taste for unhappiness that transference, with the unconscious connivance of the psychoanalyst, reproduces and maintains. Moreover, symptoms, which will take on infinite variations, must be regarded as protective forces for the voluptuous pain that the analysand does not wish to disturb or even suspect in the least. This is what others have called *jouissance*, a mixture of extreme pleasure and of suffering.

Psychoanalysis did not discover that horror is the basis—and perhaps the bedrock—of human existence. From Aeschylus to Kurosawa and Shakespeare in between, the greatest artists have said this and, doubtless, only the greatest could. The mixture of implacable destiny and cruelty has never ceased to fascinate; only this continuous fascination could elevate those artists's works to the status of universal literature. All people recognize themselves in such works, whose beauty allows spectators to temper and even forget their emotion so that this emotion retains its force without their knowing it. The originality of psychoanalysis does not lie in the fact of pointing out that human life is founded on unfathomable suffering; many others have already done that more effectively. Psychoanalysis's unprecedented originality is to have invented a laboratory where that foundation could be reproduced or produced so as to be recognized and treated.

What first appears in this laboratory is, therefore, the very opposite of the elements of an ethics. To recall the terms I have already mentioned, the forces that are revealed here or that underlie (sometimes secretly) the nonrelationship of transference are horror, voluptuous suffering, complacent self-destruction, and desubjectivation—in a word, the very antithesis of the responsibility, autonomy, liberty, and altruism to which all moral doctrines claim to lead us. And if we evoke the rules required to bring this experience to light, we are led back to the same difficulty, because those rules are constitutive, not normative.

A fundamental rule of analysis is thus to say everything without restriction, without regard for the consequences, without reserve, without respect for oneself or for anyone, without any intention and without a plan. This rule is radically opposed to the ordinary use of language in human relations. If the words spoken by the analysand were addressed to the person of the analyst, they would be unbearable or they would culminate very quickly in a severing of relations, at least if we suppose (which is a hypothesis) that those words were no longer directed at seducing, provoking, or protecting him. Through this un-speech the human relationship is ruptured, and it is that relationship which is, in principle, the aim of an ethics.

Likewise, all the rules the analyst imposes on himself or the

patient—for example, the rules of rhythm, time, and payment—
are designed only to make the experience possible; they set the
conditions for it. This is particularly true of the rule of abstinence,
the one that culminates in the prohibition on sexual relations with
patients. We are supposed to regard this as a moral rule, an aspect of the analyst's professional ethics. That, however, is not at
all the case. Although the same interdiction is applied to teachers or doctors it does not carry the same value, because it is ex-
trinsic to the practice involved in those professions whereas the
opposite occurs in analysis. Even if the failure to respect this prohibition can complicate teaching or medical care, those activities
are not intrinsically modified by it, whereas transference can be
maintained only by supposing that the sexual goal is not reached.
The very existence of the psychoanalytic relationship depends on
it: this relationship must never be situated in external reality but
rather at the level of psychic reality—that is, the level of dreams,
phantasms, and images. What this prohibition protects in analysis
is the unreality of transference. It is thus a question not of respecting a moral rule but of setting into place an element necessary to
the experience.

We cannot find the link between psychoanalysis and moral doctrine if we do not venture beyond what is intrinsic to analysis:
namely, the role it can rightfully be asked to play in relation to the
outside world, to the life of the patient outside of analysis, first of
all. In other words, morality intervenes only insofar as we raise the
question of the goals of analysis. This question is often eluded by
psychoanalysts, a great number of whom have been and perhaps
still are reluctant to take a position in regard to the psychoanalytic
cure. Clearly, the elimination of symptoms cannot be the direct
and immediate aim of analysis. The psychoanalytic method runs
counter to that quest. But this does not mean that psychoanalysis
can avoid being concerned with the well-being of the patient—that
is, with his capacity to live better as he defines it or will define it
after the experience. It is to be feared that we might be so secretly
attracted to pleasure and to horror that we are content to see them
reproduce themselves indefinitely.

However, the question we have necessarily raised is not easy to
resolve. How can we determine what living better means? How can
we decide whether the results of analysis are good or bad? For that,
we would have to have a fail-safe moral code for determining good

and evil. But where can we find one in a society that is made up of groups whose values are so frequently opposed? The psychoanalyst can do nothing more than let the analysand choose what suits him or what he cannot avoid, given his past, his possibilities, and his limits. Even then, reducing the moral doctrine of psychoanalysis to respect for the patient's choices does not allow us to transform it into an absolute and universal rule. The psychoanalyst will not be able to stop himself from passing judgment for or against the orientations adopted by his patient, whether advisedly or erroneously. No one will ever be able to provide a definite criterion for the validity of the stands he takes. The psychoanalyst knows that he can be terribly mistaken—for example (if a chance meeting allows him to confirm or correct his judgment), that he had judged as deplorable or even catastrophic something that, in the long run, turned out to have a happy ending he had never imagined.

Although curative criteria are totally lacking, in the sense that they can never be anything but individual and subjective, the fact nonetheless remains that the psychoanalytic cure—defined simply as a benefit gained from analysis—must be desired. We can, at least, give that benefit a distinct character: it only exists in relation to what is outside of the analysis, that is, in relation to its conclusion. If there is an ethics of analysis, it can only be through accepting the idea that the analysis is not everything, that it must never become self-enclosed or sufficient unto itself. Consequently, the only possible end of analysis, as a goal recognized by a moral doctrine, is its end as a time limit and as a limit in space. The moral doctrine of analysis—its most imperative ethical purpose— is to move beyond analysis and be done with it. Those who avoid the question raised by the cure do so because they want, directly or indirectly, to make analysis, and the psychoanalytic world along with it, self-enclosed. Even if, by definition, we cannot give any justification or guarantee for the results of our practice (because it takes place outside of any objectivity), we must nonetheless strive to account for it; otherwise, our work would have no purpose or meaning.

From this perspective, it is not enough to respect the rules that constitute the psychoanalytic experience: we must obey the rule that the end of the analysis is, indeed, the end, as we would obey a categorical requirement. The analysis's end, its completion, and even the possibility that it might be forgotten afterward, must be present and effective from the beginning and throughout the analysis. But in what form? The situation is paradoxical. According to the explanation I gave earlier, transference produces, in the most varied guises, not just a transference-neurosis but a state in which horror, self-destruction, cruelty, desubjectivation, and all sorts of related phenomena are complacently perpetuated. However, every individual may find the very foundations of his identity in that state (and thus be attached to it), to the extent that the most inalienable singularity lies in one's particular way of suffering. It is undoubtedly through this identity, upheld in the face of everything, that extreme suffering becomes a pleasure. This would place us at the center of moral doctrine, because it would place us at the heart of the relationship in which man arrives at his de-humanization—that is, the place where his "humanity" is born.

Is it not at the moment when the human being disintegrates into cruelty that his humanity comes to light? Human rights can only be affirmed in the places and times when they are held up to ridicule. We could not bear the captivating succession of famines, earthquakes, wars, and hostage-taking that we see in the media every day if it did not show the awakening of a human quality at the very moment when it seems to be fainting in the face of these horrors. And cultures, like intelligence and beauty, never appear more dazzling than on the day of their ruin. In all of this, humanness finds its beginnings.

Psychoanalysis takes up the question at that point. If it had nothing exterior to itself—that is, if it did not recognize that what lies outside of the time and space of sessions imposes itself upon the analysis—it would no longer be anything more than the performance of voluptuous suffering, that exercise in self-destruction in which everyone is certain to live, either as the victim or as the hero of a cause that has no substance. But how difficult it is to give immediacy to this exterior realm—the key to humanness—in an experience that is altogether oriented toward the interior! The psychoanalyst makes the insane wager (because his profession requires it) of doing everything he can to undo the ties that keep the analysand outside of the sordidness and horror of his pleasure, so that he can renew the analysand's humanity, his relationship to others and to the world.

What will be the concrete expression of this requirement, this necessity that comes from the outside world, where human animals are endowed with reason and use it well enough to survive together? The starting point of this requirement will express itself through horror at horror, disgust for disgust, and shame over complacency in the face of cruelty—that is, the cruelty that one inflicts on oneself and on others. Without this initial movement of turning away from the mud in which one had been wallowing there will be no initiation of a moral doctrine, no birth of humanness, and no beginning of the end of analysis. And how does a person turn away from that mixture of pleasure and pain? Only through the very excess of the process. As long as symptoms mask the abject foundation of the patient's existence, it remains in operation, silently maintaining those symptoms. However, when that foundation is laid bare in its most extreme form, it becomes unbearable. "Life doesn't interest me," a woman patient once told me; and she added: "If only I were ashamed of that." But then she continued: "You are only interested if things are going badly. You're a magician of unhappiness."

Even if we shudder to hear such comments, it would be ridiculous to reject them as pure projections. The analytic method leads to this place, but the psychoanalyst is also situated there. He would not have accepted that function if he were fully confident about his own humanity, and if he were not fascinated, in his own way, by the downfall of humanness. It will therefore be up to the psychoanalyst, first, to *experience* horror at horror for this particular case. The process will, however, be neither easy, in that non-knowledge conceals pleasure, nor definitive, in that it is always possible to abolish the distance the analysand has taken. Thus even a psychoanalyst who recognized in general the moral requirement that psychoanalysis be limited (which is the least one can ask of him) would not be guaranteed to accept that requirement. He must renew his refusal of horror in each particular case, and in a new light each time.

It is this refusal that activates and grounds the freedom in which all moral doctrines begin. This is a solitary act that no suggestion can produce. It provides the basis for the constitution of a subject who will learn to play with the force that is always threatening to drag him back down into either depression or megalomania. Any analysis that did not culminate in the reconstruction (and it makes no difference what name we give to the process) of a self, a consciousness, of a lucid instance that belongs to the world of representation, an instance able to invent a strategy that allows one both to hear the inhuman and to manage an existence in the world of human beings—any analysis incapable of such a reconstruction would be not only immoral, it should be considered as a failure.

If we want to moralize psychoanalysis, we must give a place to consciousness and to the self once again. The question did not come up in the days of Freud: short analyses did not have the time to devalorize or destroy those instances through which our inherent animal nature becomes reasonable and thus receptive to a moral doctrine. Patients could not even have conceived of the idea of taking psychoanalysis for an all-encompassing doctrine. The question would have been just as difficult to raise during a more recent era, when everything was directed at reacting to and polemicizing against the tendency to make psychoanalysis an orthopedic therapy, exclusively centered on the constitution of a self. But those days are over, and there is more of a risk today that all values and laws—including those of language—will be assigned to what is called the unconscious. The hasty effort to overcome a duality that is intrinsic to man is now leading psychoanalysis into impasses that it can only claim to avoid by remaining ignorant of them. We will have to rethink, for our practice, the connections between consciousness and the unconscious. This will lead to other concerns and modifications in our method, at least at certain moments of the cure. In any case, no moral doctrine could ever be founded by virtue of psychoanalysis. One can dream about the birth of *homo psychoanalyticus,* but that is only a dream, and it is high time that we awoke from it.

That is not to say that a consideration of psychoanalysis has no effect on our conception of moral doctrine. When, over a number of years, one has experienced how easy it is to invoke good reasons or reason *tout court* to justify things that fall within the realm of desire and drives, one can suppose, as Nietzsche suggested, that the rules of moral doctrine are the symbolic transposition of the things we need to survive—that is, the things we need in order to protect ourselves from others and force them to respect our space and our possessions. In that case, the respect for others advocated by our ethics is either something that the revolt of the weak has wrested from the strong or a verbal concession made by the strong to establish their domination more firmly. In other words, moral rules may be the means of avoiding the worst after observing those aspects of human nature. Not yielding in one's desires or instincts can lead nowhere except to mutual destruction.

Psychoanalysis teaches us every day that we would not be so unhappy to settle into mutual destruction, at least if we were sure of being able to outlive everyone else. But, given that there would then be nobody else to destroy and nobody to see us in our triumph, we must learn to turn this reciprocal and universal tendency toward mutual destruction into a game we can safely play with other people. Moral doctrine, which is another name for the rules of this game, would thus be necessary to allow us to establish a minimal distance from generalized cruelty. What we find fascinating is the possibility that this moral doctrine can be demolished at any moment or, to paraphrase Winnicott, that the game is always ready to change into something frightening. We are obliged to accept the fact that this horror is masked by the simulacra of civilized relations.

The end of psychoanalysis is marked by the initiation into a strategy that should allow us to recognize the warning signs of depression or megalomania, whose return indicates that the necessary distance has been abolished. It is a question of recognizing these signs in order to change their course, as one does when one tells a story to a child who is scared or throwing a tantrum. In psychoanalysis, it will sometimes be our story that we are endlessly inventing. It is then that tragedy and fatality no longer seem to cling to us and we become capable of entering into the reality that other people inhabit. What psychoanalysis can teach us is how to transform a pure power relation into a strategy for coexistence, and it is in that capacity that it can support a moral doctrine. Under those circumstances, the laboratory of cruelty ends up taking on the dimensions of a playing field.

Chapter 6
The Components of Freud's Style

At the beginning of chapter 8 of *Inhibition, Symptoms, and Anxiety*, Freud writes: "The time has come to pause and consider. What we clearly want is to find something that will tell us what anxiety really is, some criterion that will enable us to distinguish true statements about it from false ones. But this is not easy to get. Anxiety is not so simple a matter. Up till now we have arrived at nothing but contradictory views about it, none of which can, to the unprejudiced eye, be given preference over the others. I therefore propose to adopt a different procedure. I propose to assemble, quite impartially, all the facts that we know about anxiety without expecting to arrive at a fresh synthesis" (*S.E.*, 20:132). This text was written in 1926. Thus, in order to get at the essence of anxiety—a subject that had haunted him for thirty years—Freud wanted to be able to rely on the rule that lies at the heart of the most elementary, universal logic: the rule that one must distinguish things that are not identical. This is, quite simply, another formulation of the principle of noncontradiction.

Would Freud then be a philosopher? Precisely not, since he recognizes that the object with which he is dealing in this passage, anxiety, is quite difficult to subject to the rule of "either-or." And he would undoubtedly feel the same about psychoanalysis in general.

However, if he makes this comment at the beginning of this particular chapter, it is by no means in order to shield his work from falling under this rule. In fact, in the very next paragraph Freud applies that rule by wondering whether anxiety is adequately defined by displeasure. And he replies negatively with the following proof, which is a transposed form of "either-or" logic: "There are other feelings, such as tension, pain, or mourning, which have the character of unpleasure. Thus anxiety must have other distinctive features besides this quality of unpleasure" (*S.E.*, 20:132). That is, anxiety and displeasure have something in common, a zone of intersection, but each also has a zone that is uniquely its own. The two notions do not overlap.

In order for a correct definition of anxiety to be devised, one must therefore isolate the specific quality of displeasure that is proper to anxiety and belongs to it alone. That, one might say, is Freud's principal goal in this chapter, and he achieves it by applying the same fundamental rule we cited above. In fact, if we continue our reading of this text we see that he will propose a series of traits that can characterize displeasure, verifying each time whether this or that trait applies to anxiety and in what measure it applies to it alone, to the exclusion of any other affect.

In his exposition, however, Freud does not proceed in the manner of a philosopher—that is, by deduction. If you read Hegel's *Logic*, you will notice that every proposition derives from the preceding one by the necessity of the reasoning. Every proposition, whose determination carries its negation within it as its ineluctable consequence, makes it possible to establish the following proposition. This is how one progressively constructs a concept that expands out of the entire discourse that precedes it. Freudian construction, on the other hand, operates not through deduction but through successive additions, for its primary goal is to describe a phenomenon as completely as possible. Every paragraph will be entrusted with the task of introducing a new characteristic and adding it to what precedes, either by appealing to experience or by recalling general ideas developed elsewhere. The inadequacy of a characteristic makes it necessary to fit another one into the description. But this is not properly speaking a deduction, for the propositions that concern one characteristic in the series do not require Freud to derive the next characteristic out of them. That characteristic is, rather, imported from elsewhere, from the clinic or the theory he claims to have founded previously, like a hypothesis that demands to be tested and could thus be rejected.

Nor does Freud submit to the method of proof taught in the schools. Take a text by Lachelier.[1] From the beginning, you know the thesis he is going to defend. And each paragraph establishes in the first sentence the sub-thesis that will make it possible to demonstrate the main thesis; that sub-thesis then receives the proofs that will be summarized in the last sentence of the paragraph. Freud, by contrast, makes us participate in his quest; he thus begins by indicating the task he wishes to accomplish, but does not tells us where he is going to lead us and where he will be able to end up, as if he himself did not yet know before writing it. He advances toward that end in the way that waves move at high tide. In the first part of each paragraph, he ebbs toward what is behind him as a source of support, and then wins ground by formulating a new hypothesis that draws upon the preceding hypothesis through the repetition of certain words, which often acquire a new meaning as a result of the progression. He does not, however, reveal the reason underlying his movement. That reason will not become apparent until later, when the basis of the proposed solutions has been explored (before disappearing) and when the different levels of objections have been submerged.

It would take me hours to demonstrate in detail the distinctive manner of Freud's style. I refer those who are interested to an analysis of *Die Verneinung* that appeared in the third issue of the journal *Philosophie*.[2] For the present purposes, you will have to take me at my word, which is quite regrettable in a debate in which philosophers are taking part.

The only idea I can convey here is that the status of proof is displaced with this very particular form of writing. Undoubtedly, the model of "either-or" logic is never forgotten. Freud never stops working through distinctions and making objections to himself in order to reject hasty conclusions that say too much (or rather, never enough). However, this method, which is used to seek out specific difference—the difference that would, in this case, make it possible at last to devise an adequate definition of anxiety through the characterization of displeasure—and which we can label *analytical*, is tirelessly reintroduced through a movement that stems from *rhetoric*. By allowing ourselves to be carried along by the successive waves of this rising tide, we begin to think in tandem with the author and, in a certain sense, like the author. We are absorbed by the continuity of the waves; that is, we yield to the arguments, all of them so deftly critiqued and debated, and we accept the conclusions to which the text leads us, so much so that we forget the repeated doubts and hesitations. Yet it is those doubts and hesitations that measure the value of the conclusions from the viewpoint of the requirement for proof.

Are we, then, at a considerable distance from philosophy? Certainly, and without any possible question. But didn't the object of psychoanalysis make that distance ineluctable? When Freud established the unconscious as something that knows nothing of contradiction, extraposition in space, and temporal succession (he could have added sexual or individual differentiation to the list), he did so because he had listened to the discourse of madness, anxiety, and dreams, and had the audacity to want to account for that discourse in the era of science and technology. When one studies Freud's writing, one notes that this insane objective weighed heavily on him, prompting strange modifications in relation to the normal usage of the German language. To translate into his discourse psychological events that are foreign to discourse—and, as Michel Henry would say, that do not belong to the domain of representation[3]—Freud used, consciously or unconsciously, techniques of exposition that make his syntax regress toward primitive languages that are dominated by parataxis. One need only refer to certain passages in chapter 7 of *The Interpretation of Dreams* (although one could, of course, do the same demonstration using other works) to show that the repetition of words within a paragraph or series of paragraphs occurs according to a certain number of strict rules that are operative in ancient languages, Greek and Hebrew among others. Among those rules or stylistic techniques are these: concatenation (the repetition at the beginning of a paragraph of the words found at the end of the preceding paragraph), chiasmus (the repetition of a series of words in the order opposite to that of their first appearance), pericenter (the repetition at the center of a paragraph of one or several words that were at the periphery of a preceding paragraph), and so on. Through these various techniques, Freud breaks the movement that is proper to sentences in German and places all possible stress on the rhythm. Without realizing it (because the syntax grounds this rhythm in a continuous design), the reader is affected by the hammering of words whose complex interrelations simultaneously retain their meaning and open it up toward a multiplicity that can include double meaning.

Through this aspect of his style, Freud returns to the linguistic form used by primitive peoples, children, and madmen—that is, by those who are still quite close to life and who still sense that life is a rhythm that no verbal expression can truly translate. This third dimension of Freud's writing style—a style we could call *poetic*, because it reproduces the regression of the senses toward rhythm that is so characteristic of all great poetry that seeks to transmit the untransmittable quality of subjectivity's self-affirmation—is undoubtedly the most hidden element of that style, but also the most original. It is as if the founder of psychoanalysis, compelled to give voice to the inexpressible, had let himself venture so far as to invent or rediscover something that characterizes language at its inception. The results simultaneously drive language to exist in order to escape from repetition and the suffering of life, and deny language because it cannot move away from that repetition and suffering, nor even seek to forget them.

The more I read Freud, the more I am astonished that his writing conforms so exactly to his object and designs. The three dimensions I have tried to isolate—the analytical, rhetorical, and poetic—do not, of course, diminish his writing in the least; rather, they contribute to the unity of his style. Without the analytical element, Freud would have excluded himself from the domain of science, whose basic requirements are to grapple with the most extreme distinctions, to be diligent about raising ambiguities, to review and critique one's discourse constantly, and to avoid affirming something one day and its opposite at a later point, unless one underscores the modification and shows the reasons for it. In this way, Freud's effort recalls that of philosophy. However, far from marking the limits beyond which reason could not go, as Kant did, Freud sought, quite reasonably, to lift the veil of mystery covering the anxiety of the human condition so that he might, if possible, understand something about it and thereby ease it. To achieve that goal, he had to venture beyond the limits of strict reason and construct hypotheses and fictions. Then, to get this consoling creed across to his readers he drew upon the techniques of rhetoric and the art of persuasion. By that means he progressively won his readers over to his views, using the embracing resources of the German language, whose genius has taken the circular possibilities of syntax to the extreme. However, Freud wanted to go even further and was guided in that endeavor by the poets, whom he realized had already said everything he could say (and more effectively at that). He thus made his words resonate like the drums that call people forth at a dance of initiation and prepare them to become absorbed in the recounting of legends.

We psychoanalysts must, therefore, admit the truth; indeed, we should, if possible, admit it once and for all and be done with it: psychoanalytic discourse is rooted in mythology. Besides, I do not see why we defend ourselves against such a proposition, as it if were defamatory. After all, can the human mind produce anything more extraordinary than myths—that is, attempts at explaining life and the great misfortunes that punctuate and finish it? Moreover, when we know that our civilization tends to develop a mentality that should be allergic to mythologies and that, in spite of this, psychoanalysis holds a nonnegligible place within it, we should be proud to be the foot soldiers of a lost cause that we nevertheless succeed in saving. In his book *The Genealogy of Psychoanalysis*—a book that no psychoanalyst today should overlook—Michel Henry writes: "Freudian mythology has the seriousness of all mythologies, in that it arises from the same essential, secret Source that constitutes us, which is life. And that is why we believe in it without too much difficulty, because we recognize ourselves easily in it."[4] But we could not play the role of guardians of the last mythology if we took refuge in pretension in any form or failed to realize that the task incumbent upon us is infinitely complex.

If we return to this theme of mythology and compare it with the three dimensions of Freud's style we can, first of all, derive a certain number of consequences. This will allow us to characterize the style of mythology with which we are dealing in psychoanalysis. The rhetorical tale at play in our field arises from life—that is, from the mystery of affectivity and of personal suffering in the face of destiny. But this tale is constantly subject to critique by the proximity of the analytical element with which it is intertwined. If psychoanalysis can be partially defined as the critique of illusions and the process of revealing fantasies and dreams to oneself, then this critique must turn inward: that is, it absolutely must be applied to the theoretical construction, to the necessary illusion it creates through the new elaborations that are proposed to solve the enigmas of neurosis, anxieties, and death.

In other words—and this is a characteristic that separates our mythology from those of earlier centuries—this mythology must recognize itself as a mythology. As it proceeds in weaving itself, it is duty-bound to undo itself, like Penelope's handiwork; it must show itself its contradictions, its leaps, its limits, and its insufficiencies. Otherwise, it would lapse into immediate belief and become vulnerable to obcurantisms; it would become the bedfellow of tyranny in thought and action; and it would renew, in a different form, the hypnotic states it denounces. That is why it is necessary for us to open our discourse to debate and, if possible, allow philosophers to interrogate it. The advantage we will gain from this is an improved perception of the illusions into which we lapse when we claim to debunk all illusions.

It is quite difficult to base one's work on permanent critique, for that is tantamount to basing it on an ever-visible foundation of uncertainty. To avoid this, many people retreat into pretension and systematic blindness. It is, however, by means of critique that psychoanalysis remains in contact with science. By that, I do not mean the science that understands and carries out technical exploits, but rather the science that is coming into being—the science of creators. Richard Feynman, winner of the Nobel Prize in physics, said once: "What characterizes real scientists is that, whatever they're doing, they're not sure of themselves like other people are. They succeed in living with doubt. They are capable of thinking 'maybe.' They act knowing full well that it's only 'maybe.'" It is only insofar as psychoanalysis does not fear doubting its own knowledge that it can dare to call itself scientific and that it will be able to continue to think of itself as the sole mythology of the scientific age.

However, the use of reason, the concern for rigor, the requirement of clarity, and the refusal to equivocate do not function solely as constant reminders that we cannot construct anything on the basis of our mythology, or that it is not possible to deduct valuable conclusions from our hypotheses, or that scaffolds are never edifices. They also serve the purpose of returning us to real-life experience so that we can attempt a new elaboration or follow the path of regression, where the meaning of words evaporates and gives way to the sheer rhythm of life. It is by losing ourselves once again in ignorance or in the strange familiarity of anxiety that we will have the good fortune of finding a way of speaking that can correctly convey something of the particularity of those experiences.

Although our mythology must never cease to be its own enemy through its analytical dimension, it will nonetheless remain fascinating by virtue of its poetic dimension. The analytical dimension rids the poetic of its delirious quality. But the poetic dimension, in turn, invests the rhetorical with a power that it could not even imagine on its own.

Up to now, I have been discussing psychoanalysis by referring exclusively to the form it takes in readable texts. Yet psychoanalysis is not that, primarily; it is a practice. Is what I have suggested about Freud's style capable of shedding any light on that practice? In other words, is it possible to apply to practice distinctions that are made about psychoanalytic writings? I propose, by way of conclusion, to give a brief sketch of the reply that could be given to that question.

I define psychoanalytic practice as a therapy that relies on transference with a view of inducing a regression. The distinguishing feature of psychoanalysis is that it initiates its patients into the world of dreams, fantasies, and desires through a regression that is not, first and foremost, temporary, but rather topical. It is a matter of uncovering what Freud called the other scene—the scene that determines our words, our behavior, and our actions, and to which we ordinarily have no access. This is the scene of unalienable subjectivity, that is, the one where life appears as suffering— a suffering that defines singularity because the manner in which we suffer is uncommunicable, the thing to which we hold most dearly because it is the very essence of ourselves. We rejoin here the *poetic* that regresses from meaning to rhythm or, more properly, the poetic at its very inception. Isn't it the suffering of poets, their personal suffering, that compels them to write tragedies and produce odes in which they say what cannot be said?

As for transference, its effect is to cut the patient in two. By dint of paying close attention to the psychoanalyst and no attention to the outside world, the patient undergoes exactly what is produced in hypnosis: he focuses on facts and phenomena that had gone unperceived until then to the exclusion of the things that ordinarily strike the senses. This is a state of suggestion in which one allows oneself to be carried along by an un-speech that leads us to places we did not anticipate going. This corresponds rather exactly to the *rhetorical* movement of Freud's style, by which he leads his reader through the internal development of his subject, not through outside arguments but through unexpected interventions in the very course of his thought.

There remains the cure, which is difficult to define in psychoanalysis because it is not initially interested in alleviating symptoms. The goal of the cure—independence for the patient, an increase in pleasure and action, and the facilitation of communication—is, however, indispensable. Without that goal, the regression produced by transference remains in the state of naked suffering. There is no possibility of escaping from transference neurosis—that is, the reproduction of the neurosis—through the simple fact of the psychoanalytic relationship. For, in psychoanalysis, we find ourselves faced with a paradox: the regression that should set the patient free sharpens the suffering in which every individual recognizes himself as a subject and thus intensifies the refusal of the cure that would relieve that suffering. The cure must account for the fact that the method of analysis turns against it, because the cure's goal cannot help being a rejection of that suffering, or at least a distancing from it, if need be by using the anxiety that is intrinsically tied to it.

If the necessity to work toward the cure makes analysts leave the dangerous territory of initiation, it must also be imposed on transference, which would otherwise return to hypnosis. Transference only has meaning if it is limited both temporarily and topically: temporarily if it ultimately ends and gives way to autonomy, and topically if it can cease to be invasive because it has been criticized. Transforming the analyst into a master—indeed, into an intellectual guide—is tantamount to condemning oneself to never emerging from hypnosis.

This cure, you see, is nothing more than the transposition into therapy of the *analytical* aspect of Freud's style. The language used in psychoanalysis must no longer be simply an un-speech that is defined as a controlled delirium; rather, it must become a language oriented toward the outside world, that is, toward communication and intelligibility. Life is no longer merely suffering; now it seeks itself out in the realm of action and creation.

In a similar fashion, contemporary psychoanalysis has, in certain sectors, neglected to reflect upon the cure and submit to the demand for rational rigor. It cannot explain what it does to people who do not belong to its sphere in a language that is comprehensible to them, nor can it explain if and whether it can cure—that is, at least, if and how it can allow patients to live better. The two questions are fundamentally related, and one can see why the discourse of psychoanalysts is so poorly understood today; they have retreated into their mythology and make no more effort to be comprehensible in their writings than in their action.

The cure, transference, initiation—a trilogy that in my view correctly defines the components of practice—are, therefore, the equivalent of the analytical, the rhetorical, and the poetic dimensions characteristic of the style of Freud and, more broadly, of the discourse of psychoanalysis. The analytic in psychoanalysis is constantly conditioned by the poetic—that is, by the initiatory—but the initiatory must also respect the laws particular to the analytical, without trying to become similar to it. One does not make poetry when one is theorizing. Finally, it is by playing simultaneously on these three registers, in practice and in the work of elaboration on experience, that psychoanalysis can in my opinion retain its place, a place that is still necessary to our culture.

Chapter 7

On Transference Neurosis

The question I would like to raise can be formulated as follows: can we cure anyone of transference neurosis through transference neurosis? If transference is a fundamental characteristic of psychoanalysis, and if the description of this phenomenon leads us to view it as the place where neurosis is reproduced, we are going to find ourselves in a bind. In order to overcome this provoked neurosis, the transference will have to be suppressed; in that case, however, the analysis itself will have to come to an end. Freud never really found a way out of this difficulty. In fact, he proposed ideas about transference that seem quite contradictory. At some moments, he considers transference a powerful tool that allows the analyst to act for the patient's well-being, while at other moments he declares that the same transference plays into the hands of resistance; at times he presents transference as an artifact that should have a temporary purpose, while at other times he seems to regard its resolution or disappearance as being so difficult as to border on the impossible. It is as if psychoanalysis had discovered a marvelous remedy that it could subsequently no longer do without. One illness has been replaced with another that cannot be easily cured. My initial question should, therefore, be phrased differently: How is it possible to cure transference neurosis?

Before I attempt to answer this second question, I would like to linger over the term *transference neurosis*. What does it entail? Through transference, that intense affective relationship discussed by Freud, we reproduce the type or types of relationships that we maintain with others—types of relationships that are not directly or easily discernible through our behavior because they are governed by very long-forgotten experiences, both passive and active, which have been transformed into efficient phantasms. In the artifact of transference, as in a laboratory, we repeat our mode of functioning toward others in a pure state. We do so in a pure state because we are freed, on the one hand, from the reactions of other people, which force us to hide or disguise our own spontaneous actions and reactions and, on the other hand, from responsibility for our acts or words.

However, the description I have just provided reveals just one side of transference. If this were the only side present, the revelation of our mode of functioning would be devastating and we could, as sometimes happens, go mad as a result; we could also, under the effects of this vision, modify our functioning—radically, if need be.

There is another side of transference that makes it a neurosis. We are attached to our relational mode of functioning and do not wish to change anything about it. I think it is necessary to stress this point and, to grasp it fully, return to an elementary experience we generally have during our first sessions with a patient: the patient explains to us that he is suffering from a certain number of symptoms and asks us to relieve him of them—in a word, to cure him—but we soon notice that he is also asking us not to cure him of them. If the symptoms are indeed present, there are some good reasons for that; they are undoubtedly bad reasons, but good ones nonetheless, for symptoms are useful, necessary even: they have been cleverly forged to preserve a certain something to which the patient is attached, clinging, or stuck, and that he does not want to let go of. It is as if the suffering tied to his symptoms were his most precious possession, as if he would have to renounce his identity by losing it, as if, finally, his suffering, his own manner of suffering, were his singular form of existence, his only wealth.

This cultivated suffering, which is one of the characteristics of neurosis, would be totally unintelligible if we did not link it to a mode of relating to others. Preserving this suffering is the only means at our disposal to avoid separating ourselves from those who have recognized us in their very refusal to recognize us, from those whom we have imagined to be our indispensable interlocutors in order to support our own image, and from those whom we have allowed to become a part of our being and who have been destroying us in the process. This suffering that constitutes our unique way of living carries with it the ambiguity of any relationship: the ambiguity of a love that is also hate, of a rejection through absorption, of a penetration that occurs by force of exclusion. Neurosis is involved because we are incapable of doing without this suffering—in other words, because we are incapable of separating ourselves from the other who is persecuting us, for that other is also the being who establishes our existence. To phrase it in yet another way, each and every individual oscillates between the desire for independence, mastery, and responsibility, and the infantile need to return to a state of dependence, of irresponsibility, and thus of innocence.

It is this suffering in and through one's relation to another human being that will be repeated in transference. It will thus appear plainly and can thereby be treated, even though it cannot be abandoned, because it constitutes the patient's very being. Quite the contrary, if the transference prompts this suffering to repeat itself, if the transference makes it believe that it is beneficial to repeat itself, the suffering will delight in that, and the analysis will be nothing but an occasion for the patient to sink a bit deeper into neurosis, with more lucidity perhaps, but in despair over ever finding a way out. In our civilization, nothing but analysis is capable of combining the illusion of a desire that will finally become great with the bitter pains of adult infantilism.

If transference neurosis resembles what I have just described, what means do we have of getting out of it? The first response Freud gave to that question is this: if the neurotic symptoms persist, it is because they remain unconscious; if we make them become conscious, they will lose their strength and disappear. Freud was way ahead of us in discovering the limits of this position. Although recollection can, in certain cases, have positive effects on the course of analysis, it quite often happens that it gives way to repetition, more exactly to repetition via transference. The act of becoming conscious occurs by means of the release of affect. But in this case, we can no longer affirm that coming-to-consciousness was what succeeded in bringing about a transformation and freeing the patient of the symptom. Rather, it was the release that was decisive—thus, the reproduction of an emotion in an emotional register. Through this radical modification of the curative method, what shifts to the background is the ideology of the Enlightenment and its belief in the efficacy of knowledge. However, the problem posed by transference neurosis is not, for all that, resolved; for repetition in transference can remain an expression of this neurosis, and the fact that a release has taken place does not necessarily mean that the patient will not prepare himself to reproduce it on other occasions.

In order for the end of transference neurosis to occur, the psychoanalyst must lose or no longer hold his place: that is, he must no longer be the prop that upholds the standard relationship reproduced in analysis by the analysand. How is it possible for an event of this sort to happen?

To venture some kind of answer to these questions, we must first make a detour. As we know, a large part of Freud's work is based on the distinction between affect and representation. (I should note that this distinction is a commonplace of German literature and philosophy, particularly in Fichte and Schelling, who wonder how it is possible to represent the unrepresentable.) For example, Freud explains transference neurosis by the fact that the representation tied to an affect does not originally correspond to it; the analyst's task will consequently be to rediscover the representation that truly fits this affect. Freud likewise accounts for phobia by supposing a link between an affect and any representation whatsoever—and the choice of representation is so arbitrary that the analysis is unable to find a representation capable of accounting for this phobia. Freud uses a similar model to conceive of anxiety neurosis, and that is why he claims that it cannot be attacked by psychotherapy. The same is true of transference, whether it is a matter of transferences in the plural, each affect being tied to a characteristic represented by the analyst, or whether it is a matter of transference in the singular, in which case it is the entire affectivity of the patient that seeks to represent itself through the person of the analyst.

Why have I made this detour through the distinction between affect and representation?[1] I have done so because it seems to me that we could conceive of the end of analysis—and, thus, the end of transference neurosis—as the effect of the separation of affect from representation. In Freudian mythology or the mythology of German romanticism, affect seeks out representation: what is inexpressible in itself tends to express itself. And the analytic cure is, of course, developed on the basis of this model: by virtue of free association—that is, by virtue of nonintentional and unwanted speech—affect, which by definition escapes from intentionality and will,

will be able to express itself in words, even if it is only through the recounting of dreams, slips of the tongue, or jokes.

Through free association, a stroke of inspiration that draws upon certain recognized techniques of literary creation, affect moves into the world of representation. This is true or at least can be true as long as the analysis lasts. Hence the belief that if one pursues analysis over and over again, one will succeed in expressing everything about affect. Obviously, however, that is a total illusion. By definition, affect remains inexpressible, for it belongs to a different order from that of representation; it does not represent itself, even if it compels the individual to speak and pushes toward representation. This is well understood by the poets who, after the moment of inspiration and the work to which they subject it, recognize that they still haven't said anything.

If I propose that we think of the end of transference neurosis in these terms, it is because I have been led in this direction by certain signs. I have, for example, frequently observed that the end of an analysis was announcing itself through the fact that the analysand no longer felt the need to talk about himself, to express himself to another, to keep waiting for an echo of his own thoughts, desires, or plans. It is as if an interior universe had taken shape by dint of concentration, as if a center had appeared that ballasted the entire being such that the appeal for the intrusion of the other or in the other was no longer necessary, no more than the reactionary rejection of that other. Undoubtedly in this case, affect, as an expression of life, returns to itself and intensifies, affecting itself while no longer needing to be represented.

Perhaps an example will clarify what I am trying to suggest. A young woman had an incomprehensible anxiety crisis. When she tried to remember the moment when her anxiety began, she thought back to an encounter of just a few moments that she had with a man, after which she had begun to dream about having an affair with him; she was still in this state of reverie when she came to see me. Once she had succeeded in freeing herself from those thoughts, the anxiety stopped. I am well aware that an example is an inexhaustible source of misunderstandings because it can be interpreted in multiple ways. All that I want to retain is one aspect of this example: the young woman's anxiety was created by a representation that had, so to speak, brought it out of itself; this anxiety ceased when the corresponding representation was detached from it. This woman was not suffering from reminiscence, as Freud says of the hysteric; rather, she was suffering from representation.

Here is another example that psychoanalysts encounter countless times in analysis. When an analysand who has long held his parents responsible for what was happening to him succeeds in dismissing them, referring only to himself from then on and assuming the burden that weighs upon him, a complete upheaval occurs. His symptoms disappear because they are no longer tied to representatives outside of himself and because the affects that had been turned into symptoms retreat inside him, in a sense. He no longer has even to feel responsible for them; he *is* these affects.

Out of this example, I would draw the following rule: affects become pathological, that is, they turn into anxiety or symptoms, to the extent that they seek to be represented, and to the extent that rather than becoming affected themselves through concentration and nonintentionality, they become alienated through representation. One could, therefore, say that the suffering I described at the outset of this chapter as the equivalent of refusing to be cured is simply an affect that has emerged outside of itself. One cannot be cured of refusing to be cured, no more than one can make someone abandon his style of suffering, the thing that constitutes his being. What one can modify is the relation between this suffering and the world of representation. This is a form of suffering only because it tries to represent itself to itself, and thus to others; if it turns away from the mirror, the suffering turns into strength. It does not lose itself, it does not renounce itself, and it does not sacrifice itself; rather, it abandons the self and the consciousness where it had sought to see and reproduce itself—that is, a field that was not made for it.

The refusal to be cured, another name for transference neurosis, is thus transformed when the individual's unique kind of suffering, which defines his very being, becomes his unique kind of strength. I am by no means speaking here of narcissism, not even primary narcissism (or else the expression is poorly chosen). For Narcissus contemplating himself is always already projected outside of himself through his expectation of the recognition of others: he wants everyone else to be this gaze he casts upon himself. To be done with transference neurosis one must no longer need recognition, not even a self-recognition, because one is no longer in the domain of representation but rather in the domain of the affect that affects itself, or quite simply that of life, which does not need to look for any proof of itself because it constitutes its own proof. Neurotic suffering derives from the fact that affect is constantly in a state of inadequacy and consequently seeks to tie itself to representation. Affect, in its self-activation, no longer needs representation because it no longer needs to be represented, neither for itself nor for others. It has left the theater where it reveled in itself. Then there is no longer any anxious expectation as in anxiety, nor any trusting or confident expectation as in transference. What establishes itself is something like a self-hypnosis, because the affect, now returned to the dormant state in which it belongs, no longer seeks to support itself in the conscious state of representation. Because affect is now unlinked from representation, it recovers the strength that is distinct to it.

To clarify the idea I am trying to express, I will indulge in a trivial comparison: at the end of an analysis, one should no longer be an apprentice but, rather, an artisan. In order to correct his gestures, the apprentice is constantly obliged to think about each one; he thinks successively about the proper way of placing his arms, his legs, his body. This necessity to think incessantly, to watch himself acting, to reflect on the means of improving his technique will undoubtedly have positive effects later on; but, for the time being, the apprentice's own thoughts are a burden to him and take him, constantly and paradoxically, out of his body, which is now functioning like a machine that is controlled from outside. By contrast, all of those gestures have become natural for the qualified artisan; thinking about them would disturb the perfection of their accomplishment. He has internalized his art to such a point that he has liberated his inner forces, which, as in the state of hypnosis, are now freed from any conscious attention yet are nonetheless attentive to the conditions imposed by his work and uniquely occupied with carrying out his task.

On the other hand, at the end of the analysis the analysand could regard himself not as a demagogue, but as a politician. The demagogue cares only about his past and future voters and is constantly trying to conform to their expectations, but always in an awkward and untimely fashion. The politician has a goal in mind; he knows that his outcome will always come from some other secret and uncontrollable place, and that it will never be the result of the sum of the research and information he has gathered. It is as if he felt and perceived parameters that are far more numerous than he is capable of analyzing. If he is asked to explain his decisions, he will be able to give nothing but answers of this sort: I acted out of instinct. The artist says exactly the same thing to account for his work.

A number of you will certainly associate what I have just said with the practice of Zen. There is a little book that is modest but enlightening, written by a German philosophy professor named Herrigel.[2] He had been invited to spend a few years teaching in Japan, and he had taken it into his head to become initiated into Zen. Someone suggested to him that the most rapid route, and the one that would be most accessible for a foreigner, would be that of learning archery. It becomes clear as one is reading this book that the height of this art lies in the total disconnection of consciousness and any possibility of seeing oneself in the act of shooting an arrow. The master archer is the person who can hit a target at the very center in the dark and with his eyes closed. Under such circumstances, the body is turned away from any effort by the intelligence and focused on itself, so that it rediscovers the perfection of instinct. Our civilization is worlds away from such practices— most particularly the insane intellectualization of psychoanalysis. Yet psychoanalysis has everything, I think, that is needed to become the closest thing there is to Zen. It is even that, probably, which makes it so supremely seductive in our culture.

According to one current conception of analysis, the longer it lasts the greater chance we have of resolving all our problems, understanding everything, and reaching the state of transparency. It is as if we are saying: "Analysands, try it one more time." We know full well that this never happens in practice, but we think nonetheless that, in principle, there is no limit to the possibilities of analysis and that the more this limit is deferred, the greater the benefit will be. However, this is already false in theory, in the strictest Freudian sense, for however much one "makes the unconscious speak" (as they say), the unconscious can never be dissolved, since without it there would not be any sort of consciousness or humanity, either. This should serve as a warning that the belief in a principle of "the longer it lasts, the more it is worth" has something erroneous at its heart.

Our error, I think, is that we have not reflected enough about the radical difference in regimen between affect (or, if you prefer, the drive that characterizes the dynamic unconscious) and representation. Perhaps Freud, obsessed as he was by his attempt to found a science, always hoped to shift the entire unrepresentable character of affect into the field of representation, even while recognizing his failure. Hence Freud's idea to suppose representations in the unconscious, for example; hence also all of the ambiguities of the term *unconscious* and the internal contradiction of all psychoanalytic concepts.

It seems to me that we could adopt a different perspective. The work of analysis may be exhausted in this effort to represent affect. In other words, all of the representations that are acquired in analysis with a view to translating and interpreting the unconscious may turn out to stem from illusion, and the effort may culminate in renouncing all hope of understanding anything about the affect in itself, such that this field of affect closes upon itself. Renouncing representation, an act that can take place only after a long course, would be identical to renouncing being on center stage before others and before oneself—that is, to renouncing running after recognition and all forms of narcissism.

This would allow us to avoid a certain number of false problems: for example, the problem of unanalyzed elements that remain after analysis, or the problem of the unanalyzable. A remaining element is quite simply affect, which will never stop escaping analysis. It will no longer be a remaining element, but rather will be restored to its essence, to the extent that, cut off from representation, it returns to itself and is transformed into a strength through its intensification. If we do not want any more remaining elements to exist— that is, if we want transference neurosis to cease—there is only one means to accomplish it: get out of the analysis. The end of analysis must be its end; in other words, its goal must be its cessation. It is by imposing a term on the futile attempt to transform affect into representation, it is by ceasing to speak and to need to speak and express oneself, that transference neurosis will die of hunger. The analysis will then appear to be reaching the end of its course, not as a process grounded in intelligence and lucidity (which it has rightly been for a certain time), but as the process of forgetting the affect that has returned to the living body and circulates there freely to provide strength.

The psychoanalytic ideology does not wish to hear about the bodily techniques that are invading our culture today. This is understandable, given that our technique has come to consider nothing but language isolated from meaning and even more so from affect. However, if we were simply willing to go back to the traditional definition of the psyche as that which animates the living body, we would no longer have any difficulty in regarding psychoanalytic technique as something that could, at certain moments in the cure and in certain cases, take advantage of techniques which aim to draw attention to the body. Certain psychoanalysts occasionally use relaxation, but they refrain from talking about it much and from using it to ask certain questions of psychoanalysis—as if this were some shameful practice that was, in any case, totally unworthy of the purity of psychoanalysis.

Making affects return to themselves and making them circulate in the living body is not synonymous with cutting oneself off from the outside world. It is exactly the opposite that happens. The Narcissus who contemplates himself in his own mirror and in the mirror of others is so preoccupied with himself that he understands nothing about other people, nor about the multitude of events and phenomena going on around him. By contrast, the person who forgets the effort to understand himself puts all of his strength at the disposal of his action and becomes attentive to everything that can happen in his environment.

Nor does making affects return to themselves have anything to do with repression. It is the representations of the ego or superego that bind affects, separating them from each other and making them rigid. When one speaks of repression, one focuses only on the fact that a drive, an impression, or a conflict is pulled back from consciousness and from the world of representation because the individual does not want to deal with it. Yet repression is also a process of isolation. A given sensation, sentiment, or affection is cut off from the rest of the psyche and is no longer participating in the totality of its life; concentrating on it and reintroducing it into that totality is also a means of lifting the repression.

Everything that I have said here could be summed up in the following manner. If transference neurosis is necessary for the analysis to be developed, and for the thing that has been forgotten or repressed to come to the surface without being expressed, this neurosis can end only through the affect's returning to itself. Psychoanalysis should thus be understood as entailing a double movement: on the one hand, a movement that goes from affect to representation, and on the other hand, one that goes from the representation that is abandoned to the affect that leads us back to the interiority of life. Our scientific and intellectualist civilization hardly prepares us to accept, and even less to conceive of, this second movement. In the computer age it is perhaps even more difficult than before to remember that we are also animals, that our relationships are first constituted by immediate impressions, that instinct often guides us in our actions far more surely than intellectual deductions, and that we are out of touch with our era and our peers because we no longer know how to perceive and recognize the signs of their presence through any means beyond ideas and formulas. And yet psychoanalysis could, I believe, be the best place to account for, respect, and develop this other dimension of humankind.

Chapter 8

Pedagogue or Mystagogue

It might, at first glance, seem that the problem has been definitively resolved: psychoanalysis has nothing to do with pedagogy, since the psychoanalyst does not claim to lead the analysand from one point to another by following steps known in advance, nor does he impose a route on all the individuals in a group who have similar knowledge and dispositions. Pedagogy, which seeks to bring everyone to the same level of capacity, nonetheless comes up against collective and individual resistances as it accomplishes its program, and must take those resistances into account. How will it go about overcoming them? To what method will it resort in order to avoid having a given individual or group relegated to the margins of society before he or it is able to choose that place? What will it do to overcome a student's dislike for learning and even for living? How will it cure students of their disinterest? How will it inspire the desire to grow and progress? It will have to bring into play forces that cannot be itemized in books.

As for psychoanalysis, doesn't it have a goal, and doesn't it claim to help patients reach that goal through specific paths that are, by now, well known? Didn't Freud clearly define the theoretical elements in which one had to believe in order to be recognized as a disciple of the field he had formed? Wasn't psychoanalysis then—as it may still be today—the key that was supposed to open the door to the master's work, in other words, the slave that leads the children to the school? [1]

It is equally clear that medicine has nothing to do with psychoanalysis. Whereas the physician seeks to cure symptoms, the psychoanalyst is not preoccupied by them. Whereas medicine seeks to restore a past state of integrity, to return the patient to the state that preceded or should have preceded the illness, this is by no means the goal of the psychoanalyst, who anticipates something new, something that has never been seen or heard by the analysand and never accomplished by him, for he had never been able to imagine it. It is thus a question not of restoration but of discovery and, some have even said, of revolution. If, by chance, one takes a step backward in psychoanalysis, it is always in order to forestall something predictable.

However, the various goals proposed by analysis—the possibility of action or of pleasure, genital or vicarious fulfillment, learning how to play, affirming desire, gaining access to the subject's truth, working through a phantasm, and so on—can all be easily taken for definitions of the transformation, and thus of the special cure, toward which psychoanalysis is directed. (Parenthetically, we might ponder over the variety of goals that are assigned to psychoanalysis; and if we do not rush to the conclusion that the position we are defending is the only possible, the only true position, to the exclusion of all others—in other words, if we abandon a dogmatic attitude—then we are led to suggest that psychoanalysis is intrinsically linked to the idiosyncrasy of various psychoanalysts or to the era in which they presented their solution. It would then be quite difficult to reduce psychoanalysis to a single figure and keep it safely shielded from any proximity to pedagogy and healing.) I am closing that parenthesis to keep it suggestive, but I may have already sketched a contestable personal position: that psychoanalysis cannot be completely indifferent to working toward a transformation, nor to defining the path one must follow to achieve it. My provisional conclusion is this: whatever definition one gives to psychoanalysis, it will probably not be able to detach itself totally from pedagogy and medicine.

Yet wouldn't it be possible to accomplish that detachment by making psychoanalysis an initiation into the mysteries of unconscious life—that is, into the world of dreams, desire, phantasms, and drives? Under such circumstances, the psychoanalyst would become a sort of mystagogue, whose interest would be entirely focused on the experience and knowledge of realities unknown to objective science and humans in general. It would be a matter of reopening a path that the demise of religion has closed in our culture. This may, after all, be what Freud strove to do when he cited Virgil in an epigraph to his greatest masterpiece, *The Interpretation of Dreams*: *Flectere si nequeo Superos, Acheronta movebo* ("If I cannot bend the Higher Powers, I will move the Infernal Regions"; *S.E.*, 5: 608). It is true that the same sentence is quoted once again toward the end of chapter 7 and that it is explicitly referred to the glorious path of dreams, which provide knowledge of the unconscious and whose significance can thereby be reduced. On the other hand, the knowledge of the unconscious, as Freud describes it, may also repeat humanity's oldest gesture of seeking to bring to light the grand secret of existence: namely, that man is caught between the powers of heaven and hell. In any case, you will grant that Freud was not a minor erudite thinker who knew his classics, but rather a giant who had the audacity to confront the infernal powers.

However, to underscore the complexity of the problem with which we are grappling, it may also be necessary to return to the era in which psychoanalysis was born. Odo Marquard has shown in his *Schwierigkeiten mit der Geschischtsphilosophie* (*The Difficulties with the Philosophy of History*) that the philosophy of history came to replace theodicy but that reason, the master of history, recognized that it was in a state of weakness once it was left to itself in the face of nature.[2] In light of that, Freud would seem to be extremely close to the philosophy of Schelling because of the central place they both granted to nature, and because of the solution they proposed for surmounting the weakness of reason, or, more precisely, of consciousness: for Schelling, the solution would be aesthetics, and for Freud, therapeutics. Freud's vocabulary, with its reference to two systems, conscious and unconscious, to the unconscious as indeterminate and formless, to inhibition and repression, and so on, is already present in Schelling, and for the same reason: art and medicine are envisioned as a solution to the impotence of reason and of consciousness. "Aesthetics and therapeutics and their circumstances, as an organ—that is, as the symptom of a single, fundamental process—collaborate together on the philosophical valorization of the power of nature" (Marquard, 90). After having thought that "every force of salvation resided solely in nature" (Marquard, 92), German Romanticism—which culminated with Freud, among others—did not fail to realize that nature contained a threat. The art of genius and the art of care therefore took on the role of trying to save mankind from this savior. Yet the failure of aesthetics in transforming reality so as to overcome nature's dangerous aspect led philosophers to take an interest in medicine and physicians to take up philosophy. Throughout the nineteenth century, the exchange between medicine and aesthetics was pursued. On the one hand, literature was invaded by the figures of the physician and the patient; on the other hand, thinkers became more and more interested in the link between genius and madness. Aesthetic production became a substitute for therapy.

Freud joined Schelling in affirming that the process of anamnesis was central—central to therapy for the former, and to aesthetics for the latter. They also both produced a theory of sublimation on the basis of drives inhibited by nature.

The same cultural context tied together pedagogy and aesthetics. One need only recall the book by Schiller, so typical of this period, entitled *Über die aesthetische Erziehung des Menschen* (*Letters on the Aesthetic Education of Mankind*). Or one might recall Goethe's *Wilhelm Meister*, or, to go even further back to a work that undoubtedly served as Goethe's model, the highly successful novel by Moritz, whose title is suggestive: *Anton Reiser, ein psychologischer Roman* (*Anton Reiser, a Psychological Novel*). The point is to show the constant interplay that was established during this era between literature, education, and psychology.

What can we find interesting about these connections? If psychoanalysis was indeed born in this cultural context, then it may remain marked by it, and the same exchanges and interactions between the various disciplines may continue to occur today. It may not be so easy to mark definite boundaries between them.

Undoubtedly, the proximity of psychoanalysis to aesthetics does not bother us; to the contrary, aesthetics ennobles our field, and we don't wish to do anything to exclude it. We gladly remember that Freud never renounced having read Goethe and that he was familiar with the poets, who, he believed, already knew all the ideas he was able to propose and had even surpassed him. Freud compared case histories to novellas and, coming from his pen, they often take on the air of a novella.

On the other hand, we are ready to take our distance from medicine, not only because of its direct concern with healing but because it is coming more and more to resemble the exact sciences. However, even though Freud sought to keep physicians from monopolizing psychoanalysis, he did not exclude them from his discovery. What he wanted to avoid was having psychoanalysis reduced to a branch of medicine.

It would, however, still be possible to adopt a position of radical exclusion of psychoanalysis in regard to pedagogy and medicine. Harold Bloom, the greatest American literary critic, wrote some time ago in the *New York Times* that it is possible that Freud's importance for our culture is continuing to grow almost in direct proportion to the decline of psychoanalysis as a therapy. For Bloom, Freud's conceptions are so sumptuous in their indetermination that they are beginning to blend into our culture; indeed, Bloom posits that they now constitute the only Western mythology that contemporary intellectuals have in common. As with any true mythology, he continues, a diffuse version of psychoanalysis is becoming the common possession of most people in the middle class of Western society, people who may not be notoriously intellectual, and who undoubtedly are not always conscious of the fact that psychoanalysis has furnished the psychology in which they can believe without continuous reflection and without a conscious effort.

But, if this is the case, then why wouldn't psychoanalysts be the best mystagogues—that is, those best placed for introducing others to this mythology? This would raise a crucial question: are we, as psychoanalysts, the people who lead patients to adopt Freudian myths or the Kleinian, Winnicottian, Bionian, or Lacanian myths that followed Freud's? Or rather, are we ourselves mythmakers—indeed, are we there to allow our analysands to discover or create their own myths, those that will give, if not a meaning, then at least a grounding to their existence? Although the word "therapist" comes from the Greek word *thérapeutès*, which signifies "he who takes care" but also "servant of a god," there is another word that is very close in meaning: *thérapôn*, which also means "he who takes care" and "servant"; however, in the Homeric hymns, thérapôn refers to the servant of the Muses, whereas in Pindar it means servant of the gods. If we do not want to consider ourselves therapists, might we perhaps accept to be called thérapônes, those who listen to what comes to them from far away or on high?

There must be a link between the therapist and the thérapône. Isn't the act of listening to the muses or the gods over the course of an analysis a way of preparing oneself for something that could be seen as the reverse of the invention of a myth: that is, nothing less than the creation or re-creation of a human existence? The psychoanalyst would then be not just a mystagogue but a demiurge, unless he must join, in his own way, the band of those whom

Freud said practiced "impossible" professions (*S.E.*, 23:248). But that would probably be exactly the same thing.

The adage cited by Freud entailed three terms: governing, educating, and healing. The last term was replaced later by "psychoanalyzing." We find ourselves here at the heart of the question raised by this colloquium on psychoanalysis and pedagogy. I would couch that question in the following manner: what do these three or four terms have in common? And what does psychoanalyzing have to do with governing, educating, or healing? From what point of view is it possible to connect them? And what would be the ultimate justification for their project?

At one end of Brasilia, one can read this sentence from Kubitscheck on the monument that is dedicated to his memory: "Everything is transformed into dawn in this city that is rising for tomorrow." The dawn that is rising for tomorrow emerges out of the night—that is, out of the die that had been cast, the peremptory condemnation, the warranted discredit, the decipherable results, the sure diagnosis. Governing, but also educating and healing, imply that one is not obsessed by what is most patent, most manifestly visible or inevitable, but rather that one can sense and imagine something possible that, up to that point and for other people—perhaps for everyone—had been only the face of the impossible. It means having a gaze that does not settle for the well-established and verified reports concerning a people, a child, a patient, but rather perceives, on the margins or beneath the surface, other traits that have been almost entirely erased, other buried elements, another story, other suppressed forces. It is on the basis of these anchoring points that the work of the imagination can be performed, that a remodeling of the overall vision will be achieved, and thus that the unimaginable and impossible, imperturbably deduced from the facts, will give way to the imaginable and the possible, because something new will have been imagined as capable of becoming real.

"Power to the imagination," some have declared. It is, indeed, a question of that. But the politician, the educator, and the analyst who change necessity in history have nothing in common with the demagogue who seeks to make others believe that anything is possible and that everyone can do everything. The demagogue is someone who throws a veil of illusion over reality to keep it from being seen in its nakedness and complexity. Or he may be a pretentious person who, in fulfilling his function, identifies with infantile omnipotence. Nothing else can result from this avoidance than a repetition of the same errors and the same misfortunes. Seducing an audience by evoking Psychoanalysis with a capital *P* as the means of overseeing the eventual transformation of the social bond, or blindly obeying the professional rule that everyone should say everything, to anyone at all, is tantamount to lulling others into a delusory expectation for a future that has not come about. Imaginative work, which is always precise, limited, and risky, cannot be confused with the establishment of a vague dream or an erroneous program, which can excite people for a short time but in the end debilitates them rather than arouses them.

By the same token, that which is imaginable and possible can never emerge from a political ideology, nor from a preestablished pedagogy, nor from psychoanalysis books. A set of rules aimed at creating something can never be derived from any of that. There is a secret to imaginative work even for the person who is directly involved. Corpora of doctrines have the same effect as demagogy when one wants to use them and put them into practice: rather than producing the possibility of a future, they generate corporate or partisan regressions and a definitive marginalization vis-à-vis accepted opinion. The reason for this is simple: rather than drawing the singularity of this people, this student, or this patient out of its shell, which would be the goal of the operation, one either immerses them in a generalized sea of good feelings and good sentiments, or one forces them to accept ready-made patterns that don't fit reality.

It is not a question of dreaming or of promising anything at all, any more than it is a question of placing a vague and generous faith in the other person or of letting oneself get carried away by the first inspiration that comes along. Rather, one must plunge into a long debate with the people, the student, or the patient, explore obscure nether regions, confront violence, and open oneself up to burdens and pains without being sure of the outcome—that is, without knowing whether a new construction, a unpredicted imagination, a viable path will emerge.

If imagination is also the power of imagination (*Einbildungskraft*), it is because it is created by a process of moving forward in the midst of unrecognized powers, of abandoning, while in their midst or while in contact with them, any facile sense of superiority, or of losing a knowledge that is worn out and forced to dig down into its foundations. Imagination and its power emerge from journeys through the night, from communication that has become impossible in the heart of the closest proximity, from paths used by dreams to tame the violence of sex and death. It is under the surface of the obvious that imagination draws its energies, from the daily collapsing of past proofs and assurances. Jacqueline Picasso recounted that Pablo Picasso, who was then her husband, awoke every morning convinced that he would never paint again and then, having taken hours to work through his despair, was possessed every evening by a frenzy to paint. To paint one last time. How can we know when the possible will return? When power comes to the imagination, it is by surprise, at the moment when one no longer expects it. And if this power can be transmitted, if it can be the start of an unprecedented image and a new order for the other person, that is simply because it returns to its source: the relation to this other in which one had become lost—the "that," the crowd, the child, or the patient.

By underscoring that invention is at the heart of the task of the pedagogue or of the healer, as it is for that of the analyst because they are all the servants of the Muses or of the gods, I do not mean to imply that these functions are identical. The difference lies, first of all, in the fact that one can suitably practice education (because the role of teaching is considerable in that field) or medicine (because the application of knowledge is decisive in that field) but that, without invention, one cannot be a psychoanalyst. One can assume the role, undoubtedly, but none of the things that constitute psychoanalysis will occur. Of these various professions, it is thus psychoanalysis that allows and obliges us to extract and isolate the determining factor. An educator can excite and arouse his students without ever having to ask himself about the source of his action. He then quite simply transmits, without saying or knowing so, the passion and arousal that possess him. One can likewise be a physician who transmits the means and the power to fight illness without having the slightest need to question or wonder about that power. Such an ignorance of the determining factor is impossible in psychoanalysis, because the entire work of analysis rests on it, consists in it, because there is no visible matter on which one can lean, because the light of consciousness has been extinguished, and because the process takes place in the darkness of nonintentionality and nonwill.

Where does the difference between pedagogy and psychoanalysis lie? It is not necessary to locate it in the respective aims of each field. Obviously, one can restrict the goal of pedagogy to the acquisition of knowledge or to the training of an individual in keeping with the average standards accepted by a given society. It then becomes possible to contrast that definition with the definition of psychoanalysis as a field intent on helping the patient attain his desire, his truth, his liberation. But it is not clear that one needs to reduce the significance of a related undertaking in order to build up one's own. Let us rather suppose that the enlightened pedagogue is able to provide his students with the same services as does a therapist. It is clear that some teachers have, through their style of teaching, kept certain adolescents from falling into the hands of psychologists. And, undoubtedly, if the function of the teacher were not so undervalued in our society, there would be less need to resort to therapists in academic institutions.

Let us suppose then that the pedagogue aims at the same sort of invention as does the psychoanalyst. Where they diverge is in the means they use to achieve that end. The psychoanalyst will attempt to achieve it by lifting repressions, by setting resistances aside, by bringing forth phantasms or drives—in short, by making available to the patient powers that will allow him to live more intensely. If the pedagogue, in the best of cases, has the same goals, he will not, in contrast to the psychoanalyst, linger over the feelings or thoughts of the person placed in his charge but rather act through the intermediary of a clear project that has to be accomplished: namely, the apprenticeship in a precise discipline. He will not direct the student's attention to his resistances or phantasms but rather act upon them or put them to the test, without being in the least preoccupied by them.

And yet, things may be even more complicated. In a way, the psychoanalyst also acts indirectly. What matters for him is to succeed in liberating speech as fully as possible. He is not interested in drawing the patient's attention to his resistances, his repressions, his phantasms, or his drives. That, as everyone knows, would have the opposite effect of what is sought. It would inhibit rather than facilitate speech. It is not only when we are dealing with psychotics that we must use a medium. We know, for example, that Winnicott used sketching as much as speech to accomplish his cures. Wasn't he, in the process, very close to what can be most successful in pedagogy?

Perhaps what differentiates psychoanalysis from pedagogy is that one doesn't learn anything through the former. When Lacan defined interpretation as enigma and repetition wasn't he suggesting that, if an interpretation can have an effect, it is by provoking in the analysand not a form of knowledge and clarification but, quite to the contrary, a state of confusion that he will work his way out of by setting in play powers of which he was ignorant, and of which he had to be ignorant in order for them to remain efficient powers? If it is standard practice in psychoanalysis for understanding to come (or be believed to come) after the fact, that is because it could not precede nor even accompany the action.

The question that I would like to raise, by way of conclusion, is the following: are we not obliged to distinguish carefully between the "knowledge" side of psychoanalysis and the "effectiveness" side? In other words, are these two sides of psychoanalysis compatible, or are they destined to enter into conflict? When, at the end of an analysis, a patient reflects upon the discoveries he may have made, he may have many things to say. However, if he reflects on the changes that have occurred in his existence, he may be much less talkative. It is not rare for a patient to be unable, in the end, to say anything about what has happened and how or why those changes have taken place. I think that one could even say in general that any true transformation occurs unbeknownst to the patient, or else it is not a serious change. That means that effectiveness in psychoanalysis is independent of knowledge. Effectiveness can only take place if one has succeeded in proposing a detour that mobilizes the forces capable of leading the analysand toward an increased state of action, pleasure, and invention.

The knowledge that results from this is probably not of the order of rational intelligence. I suggested earlier that the renewal of an existence was the reverse side of the invention of a myth. It is in this register, undoubtedly, that we should inscribe analytic discourse. When we try to put the writings of the greatest psychoanalysts, beginning with those of Freud, to the test of a rational critique, they seem at best filled with unsurmountable contradictions. But that is not bothersome if what we expect from them is not an explanation but, rather, the evocation or figuration of the powers that rule our lives, and if those evocations or figurations succeed in some measure in moving the Infernal Regions further away.

I have tried, as much as possible, to shuffle the cards I was dealt when I was asked to speak at this colloquium on psychoanalysis and pedagogy. It was, no doubt, merely a game. But do you think it is possible to do anything other than play? Politics is a game, undoubtedly derisory at times; pedagogy is a game, which teachers don't always find amusing; and healing is simply a means of making it possible to enjoy one's existence, so that the necessity of destiny can be momentarily weakened. Why, then, wouldn't psychoanalysis be a game designed to keep us from falling into boredom? We could invent turns and detours for each person that disconcert him and distract him from his symptoms; and if, by chance, we happened to be possessed by some music, the *thérapône* within us would be authorized to rejoin the rhapsodists and tell some pretty story.

Chapter 9

Transmitting Anxiety

To speak about transmission in the context of psychoanalysis, we must raise a series of elementary, and therefore daunting, questions that probably have no true solution. Among other things, we must ask: What is to be transmitted and how can it be transmitted? Is it possible to transmit it? Indeed, is it legitimate to transmit it?

For example, if we try to answer the first question, "What does psychoanalysis transmit?" we can imagine varied responses. If we see psychoanalysis primarily as an experience, we will have to try to describe the specificity of this experience, striving, for example, to characterize it as an experience of the unconscious. We must then explain what we mean by that word.

At the other extreme, it may, however, be legitimate to think of psychoanalysis as a science. A certain number of psychoanalysts in France today fearlessly make such a claim. It then becomes necessary to explain what we mean by science in this particular case. That will probably lead us very quickly to describe psychoanalysis as the science of the unconscious, placing emphasis on the mechanisms that supposedly characterize the unconscious. Whether we view analysis primarily as an experience or primarily as a science, we will, I think, find ourselves asking the following question: What, then, is this unconscious whose experience or knowledge we seek to transmit? Let us, therefore, try once more to answer that question.

If we refer to the corpus of Freud's writings, two very different meanings of the term *unconscious* stand out. It is defined, first, as it was well before psychoanalysis and since it, in relation to memory. What we have in our memory is not presently conscious, so it is in that sense unconscious. Certainly we cannot overlook the distinction Freud makes between memories that are already available to consciousness and thus form the preconscious, and memories that escape consciousness entirely under the ordinary conditions of recollection and thus form the unconscious properly speaking. It is the latter sense of unconscious I am talking about in relation to memory. But, according to the second meaning one finds in Freud, the unconscious is also defined in a dynamic manner, in relation to drives and affects.

Freud would have liked the analytic experience to be limited to coming to consciousness in the form of recollection. But he was increasingly obliged to acknowledge that the patient in analysis quite often tends not to recollect, but to repeat. The process of becoming-conscious then took the inevitable form of the discharge of an impulse-quantum experienced through an affect. The analytic cure could consequently be said to unfold solely in the mode of recollection, on one condition: that the unconscious be defined only in the form of memory, even if it is memory of the oldest perceptive traces. In other words, the cure can be characterized in this way on the condition that the unconscious be formed only by the process of forgetting or repressing perceptions that were once conscious or preconscious.

If the cure cannot be limited to recollection, it is because the unconscious has this second, dynamic sense of a repressed primary drive, which has never been repressed because it has never been conscious, and because a drive is, by definition, inaccessible to any knowledge whatsoever and can be perceived only in the form of an affect—that is, of feeling.

There is, it seems to me, a confusion pervading our comments on the analytic experience, because this elementary distinction tends to be overlooked. When, for example, we speak of a knowledge that does not know itself, we are acting as if the two definitions of the unconscious were one and the same. In reality, this expression contains two meanings that are truly opposed to each other. Saying that the memory-unconscious is a knowledge that does not know itself signifies that, under favorable conditions, whether spontaneous or provoked, this knowledge that does not know itself could know itself. But saying that the drive-unconscious is a knowledge that does not know itself should signify that this knowledge will never take place—that is, that this knowledge does not exist and that the term *knowledge* creates an illusion in this case, unless one wants to maintain, in more than a metaphoric way, that the experience of the discharge of affect engenders a kind of knowledge. If that were so, one would have to attribute a kind of knowledge to animals.

By maintaining the ambiguity of the term *unconscious* and neglecting to bring that ambiguity to light, we leave the door open to the constitution of psychoanalysis as a science, thereby introducing a possibility for its transmission. But in reality we have simply created a confusion that will have fatal consequences both on the level of theory and on that of practice.

If the unconscious could be reduced to memory-unconscious, first, Freud would have brought nothing new into the field of culture, and second, the problem of transmission would not arise.

On the other hand, drive-unconscious poses a problem for transmission because it does not in the least belong to the order of consciousness, and because the term *unconscious* does not suit it. In fact, in contrast to what happens for memory, drive-unconscious is not defined in relation to consciousness. This mode of unconscious, if we want to retain the term, is transmitted in the way that one transmits life, which raises very different problems.

Can we go a step further in this direction? Drives, as Maurice Dayan has written, are tied to the living body.[1] They arise from the psyche, understood in the Aristotelian sense that was embraced by medieval thinkers and German philosophers alike: that is, as the soul that animates the living body. If we follow this tradition, the psyche does not have to be defined in relation to consciousness; rather it belongs to the living order, which is the level at which we should approach the most difficult aspects of the transmission of psychoanalysis. Freud, who like other scholars of his day followed Cartesian tradition and for whom any thought is either conscious or not, found himself obliged to admit the following in order to account for his object: psychic phenomena are not only conscious, but also unconscious. In reality, the philosophers of the tradition that goes from Aristotle to Hegel never said anything of the sort. For them, the problem was the reverse. What posed a difficulty for them was having to conceive of a conscious psychic order, because the psyche that animates the living body could in no way belong to the realm of consciousness. If we follow this route, we could, therefore, dispense with the opposition between the conscious and unconscious, and focus instead on the distinction between a psychic force that animates the living body and consciousness, which by definition includes the unconscious. It is in this sense that I will henceforth use the terms *psyche* and *consciousness*.

What could be the purpose of this change in vocabulary? It may, in a way, make our task more difficult by preventing us from shifting surreptitiously from one meaning of the word *unconscious* to another and believing that we have resolved such a crucial problem of psychoanalysis, when we have done nothing more than play on words. Moreover, this change may, I think, allow us to describe the phenomenon of transference in a different way, and to rediscover, underneath the intellectualization that is always so prolific in psychoanalysis, the part of our relationships that arises from animality—that is, from everything connected to the immediacy of the interior of the living body and of interactions between living bodies.

It would, for example, become clear that transmission in psychoanalysis must take place in two utterly different modes: one that involves the psyche, and one that involves consciousness. I do not want to describe these two modes as separate, for that would force us to go into preliminary explanations that would be far too lengthy. Rather, I will try to focus on what constitutes the pivot between these two fields: anxiety.

As you know, Freud wrote a great deal on anxiety, and his conception of it underwent considerable transformations over time. As early as 1895, he separated "from neurasthenia a certain symptomatic complex under the name 'anxiety neurosis'" (*S.E.*, 3:90). For Freud, therefore, anxiety is the expression of an excess of libido that cannot be diverted—that is, that cannot be transformed by a passage through representations. It is thus a deeply felt expression of the purely psychic. Freud vacillates between two positions. On the one hand, he explains that the affect of anxiety "is not reducible to an anterior state, just as it is not treatable through psychotherapy" (*S.E.*, 3:97); in other words, one cannot be cured of it, because it resists any substitution in the world of representation. On the other hand, Freud admits that phobias and obsessional neurosis are reactions of protection from neurosis anxiety.

In his *Introductory Lectures on Psychoanalysis*, Freud sticks to approximately the same conception. Here, he describes the state of anxiety as a primary state, which stems from an excess of libido that could not be transformed. Anxiety does not, however, manifest itself as such when it is replaced by symptoms. "Anguish is therefore the universally current coinage for which *any* affective impulse is or can be exchanged if the ideational content attached to it is subjected to repression" (*S.E.*, 16: 403–4; Freud's emphasis).

Anxiety is thus the expression of the psychic in the pure state, in relation to consciousness. Because consciousness wants to master the psyche that animates the living body, that psyche can no longer function for itself; it is required to enter into an area that is no longer its own, and it makes its presence felt in the pure form of an uncontrolled dynamism or of forces that are unleashed without any goal or direction. These are life forces, in particular sexual forces, which have taken leave of their senses and are, as it were, insane by the time they reach the field of consciousness. They therefore end up perturbing the functioning of consciousness, thus producing dysfunctions that are equivalent to symptoms. But these forces should not be confused with symptoms; in their essence they cannot be assimilated or known by consciousness, and thus could not be subjected to a treatment that originates in consciousness.

One can certainly undertake a psychotherapy of symptoms. But it is easy to understand that such a psychotherapy could reach its goal only if one leads those symptoms back to their origin: that is, to the anxiety from which they emerged. Symptoms are nothing more than solidified traces of the passage of the psychic realm into consciousness in the form of anxiety. Consciousness has sapped the anxiety of a portion of its strength, but in the process it has cut the anxiety off from its source. The symptom then becomes a partial, lifeless residue in the field of consciousness. By bringing the symptom back to the anxiety, psychotherapy forces it out of its isolation and reinvigorates it, but loses the ability to use it directly; it loses the power to control and exploit it. It is life that reasserts its rights and demands.

Transmitting anxiety therefore signifies, first of all, transmitting the life that has been fragmented and destroyed by symptoms. Anxiety is thus the process required to return to the psyche that animates the living body. But can one transmit anxiety, properly speaking?

To determine that, we must ask ourselves how exactly the anxiety that had been previously avoided through the production of symptoms reappears in the analysand, and what that supposes on the part of the analyst. The important thing is not so much that the symptom speaks and that one may, if one knows its dialect, interpret what it says. Quite the contrary, the key is to learn the tricks and detours that allow the symptom to return to the totality of the psyche—that is, to restore the symptom to the general circulation of psychic life, by drawing it out of the narrow cyst in which it had become trapped in consciousness and making it available to the psyche once again. However, this operation can take place only if the psychoanalyst does not participate in it and is not familiar with the anxiety, for the anxiety obscures his own certainties and knowledge to make room for the circulation of all possibilities. Freud was undoubtedly referring to an elementary experience of this sort when he advised analysts to forget everything in order to be able to listen to a patient—or, to cite another example, when he explained that the patient's unconscious had to communicate with the psychoanalyst's unconscious for the latter to be able to formulate what was at stake. These various passages never occur without anxiety; it is anxiety that is the crucible of analytic communication and thus of the transmission and elaboration of the experience. The renewal of the experience is achieved via anxiety, because anxiety is the obligatory pathway for returning to the living totality of psychic existence. "Anxiety is always present," wrote Kierkegaard, "as the possibility of a new state."[2]

Transmitting anxiety thus takes on a second meaning. As Kierkegaard describes it, anxiety is the possibility for freedom; it *is* freedom as a possible condition. What possible purpose could evoking freedom serve in the field of analysis? This is a question that must be raised from the very beginning, since the mere expression of such a preoccupation will surely make the most learned readers smirk. Those readers might argue that the practice of analysis does and should confine itself, through the play of free association, to bringing the events of the past back to consciousness in order to make them available for interpretation. It is not, such people maintain, a question of pondering over consequences; they will always be good, since prolonged psychoanalysis always advances toward desire and truth. I will leave those readers to their beliefs, asking instead whether, in certain cases, the laissez-faire processes of dreams, phantasms, and speech might not culminate in a kind of dissolution of thought and of existence. How could it not be possible that, by turning indefinitely and exclusively toward the psyche, as I have defined it, consciousness—that is, ultimately, the mind of man—might be torn to shreds?

What psychoanalysis produces, and what makes it invaluable, is the return of the psyche to the dream state. "In this state," Hegel writes, "the human soul [that is, the psyche] is not filled simply with separated, singular affections but, more than is the case ordinarily in the distractions of the wakened soul, attains a profound and powerful sense of its total individual nature, of the complete circle of its past, present and future, and this experience of the coming-into-being of the individual totality of the soul is precisely the reason why one must deal with the dream when studying the soul that has the feeling of itself."[3] It is from this state that anxiety arises, because this experience opens onto a possibility without any determination. If man were merely an animal, the psyche would fulfill its function of animating the living body in this state and set the instincts in motion. But, since consciousness remains present and active in this state, it finds itself without an object, or to use an expression from Kierkegaard, it finds itself faced with an object that is nothingness—that is, pure possibility. And this pure possibility without object is nothing other than anxiety; it is freedom as a possible condition. "Freedom's possibility is not the ability to choose the good or the evil. . . . The possibility is to be able."[4] It is power.

Whereas the symptom had to be brought back to the psyche through the mediation of anxiety, freedom is, for the psyche, the possibility of leaving its dream and its innocence in order to enter into the world of objects and tasks. Anxiety marks the moment when the psyche that determines the individual poses as an individual and thus as separate. In itself, the psyche—as Freud said of the unconscious—knows nothing of contradiction, temporality, and spatial relations, and thus knows nothing of the distinction between interior and exterior. It is in an immediate relationship with everything, and although it is particular, it establishes nothing individual or distinct. Anxiety appears when, under the pressure of consciousness, the psyche is forced to define itself. Anxiety is then merely separation anxiety, the anxiety of the individual who is no longer guided by instinct, nor by the mother who carries him, nor by the genius that inspires him as in a dream.

This separation of the psyche posing as something exterior to itself changes instantaneously into guilt. In the anxiety in which the individual experiences himself as the possibility for freedom, there lurks the irremediable guilt of having failed in life, of having left, even if only slightly, the psychic field of immediate communication, the guilt of having no means of achieving extraposition (expressing his solitude to the outside world) or succession.

Psychoanalysis encounters guilt at every juncture in its practice; but it will not be able to understand anything or do anything about it as long as it has not connected that guilt to anxiety as the possibility for freedom—that is, as long as it has not turned that guilt away from the past where it is stuck and toward the absolute possibility of a future, experienced in separation anxiety as a pure possibility.

According to this second meaning, therefore, transmitting anxiety signifies transmitting the possibility for freedom. This implies as a condition that, on the one hand, the psychoanalyst not be caught in the immediacy of relation, and on the other, that he not limit himself to arousing the evocation of the past. The explicit psychoanalytic technique is most often concerned with nothing more than recollection and its interpretation; such a concern is supposed automatically to produce a certain number of transformations and restructurings. Yet there could be no transformations and restructurings on the side of the patient if, on the side of the analyst, anxiety was not directed toward the future and was not the site for inventing the means of appealing to the psyche and inciting it to emerge out of its restful dream state. Is it not possible to think that, if we don't happen to know what to do with the patient's anxiety or with our own anxiety, that is because the dominant analytic ideology provides us with no instructions for imagining, conceiving, and realizing a future? One might even say that it pushes us in exactly the opposite direction.

If anxiety creates a separation, or if it is the result of the separation that forms the individual, it can also be, once again, a chance for the psyche to concentrate on itself. Anxiety shows the consciousness that the psyche hides within itself an autonomous and assured mode of functioning. It is like an envelope that closes the psyche on itself, that separates it from consciousness and especially from any other consciousness that would place it outside of itself. Within each of us there remains a possibility for psychosis, maintaining it in a relationship to another person who alienates it and is capable of entering and leaving it to manipulate it as he pleases.

This is what anxiety can bring to an end when it assumes the form of separation anxiety, but of a kind that is experienced on the side of freedom—that is, of pure possibility, of pure power, of strength.

A transference that does not come to an end, that changes from a transference onto the analyst into a transference onto his or her supervisor and then into a transference onto the analytic institution or onto a figure of uncontested master, such an incomplete transference reflects our difficulty in liberating ourselves from that backdrop of psychosis, through which we forbid ourselves to reach the beginning of freedom and thereby flee from the horror of separation that would sign our solitude. As long as transference remains, we are drawn to the all-powerful Other from whom we demand recognition. With the kind of anxiety that is power, however, a closure is achieved. The analysand doesn't yet need to speak, to express himself, to confide, to have himself supported, and the analyst doesn't need to cure himself of his uncertainty of existing while pursuing the analysis. The anxiety of solitude will become the possibility for communication.

It is in fact the obligatory site of passage—a passage that must always be repeated—which closes the psyche onto itself and spares it from megalomania. It protects the psyche from alienating intrusions because it is the border that maintains difference and thus alterity. It removes infinite narcissistic expansion because it is, to adapt a term from Freud, anxious expectation; that is, it is turned toward the presence of objects and of others. From the moment it sensed its power, a gentle anxiety emerged to concentrate the psyche on itself and open it to the outside world by virtue of consciousness, which can then reassume its limited but necessary rights.

Transmitting anxiety in its third sense thus means transmitting the end of transference and the end of the analysis. If the analysis continues, it is simply to avoid both anxiety as the possibility of freedom that projects itself toward the future and the anxiety of solitude, the kind in which certainties are always null and void. If the analysis continues, it is so that the analysand can maintain the illusion that an indefinite search will at last provide the solution, and that it will be able to combine the necessities of existence with the irresponsibility of the fetus in its mother's womb. The entire analytic ideology is probably suspended in this nonending. On the side of the analyst, the corollary to the transmission of anxiety in its third sense will be the possibility of bringing his work as analyst to an end. The sine qua non of the transmission of analysis, if it involves transmission of this last kind of anxiety, is the possibility of ceasing to transmit it. For needing to be an analyst always supposes that one needs another to cure oneself of loneliness: that is, of the fear of still not being sufficiently differentiated to exist as a distinct individual or conversely, of the fear of having to confront this irremediable differentiation. Transmitting psychoanalysis, finally, means neither needing or caring to transmit it.

Chapter 10

On the End of Analysis and
Self-Hypnosis as a Cure

> I want my activity to be that sort of inertia which works. . . .
> Being has nothing to do with something that thinks or con-
> ceives of itself as existing. It is conception that has lost every-
> thing.
>
> A. Artaud (*Oeuvres* 12:49)

During a trip with Freud, Jung told him the dream he had had the
night before, and they tried to figure out what it meant together.
Afterward, he asked Freud to submit to the same experience. Freud
shied away from the proposition on the pretext that, ever since his
falling out with Fliess—that is, since the end of what was his own
analysis—he no longer felt the need to talk about himself. Because
Jung was competing with Freud and trying to put him in a situation of equal, he reacted to this refusal with a certain bitterness,
concluding that Freud wanted at all costs to cloak himself in mystery so as to avoid the risk of falling out of his position of master.
Isn't it possible, however, to interpret this episode in very different
terms? Couldn't Freud's attitude give us some valuable information
on the nature of the end of analysis?

When, over the course of many years, we have tried time and
time again to understand the ins and outs of our history, or when
we have constructed multiple interpretations on the basis of our
dreams or various behaviors, we reach the point of being certain
that we can go no further and that it is time to close Pandora's
box. It is as if psychoanalysis were made to wear out meaning and

returned in the end to the thing—that is, to the living being that constitutes us. But, to understand how this sort of ending is possible, we have to go back to the beginning.

Some contemporary psychoanalysts repeat, no doubt with a certain measure of truth, that one must not respond to the demand of the patient. But which demand are we talking about here: the patient's demand that his symptoms be relieved, or the demand to know why those symptoms exist? While it is obvious that psychoanalysis does not deal directly with symptoms, as a doctor can and must do for bodily symptoms, it is no less obvious that it must account for the existence of those symptoms. It is true that the first demand is explicit, whereas the second usually remains implicit. Or at least it is often implicit for the patient, who, having never undergone analysis, does not have a clear idea of why he is attached to his suffering. However, from the very first session a reasonably well-informed psychoanalyst can easily read between the lines and hear this demand.

We would, therefore, be quite mistaken not to account for the patient's demand—even the first explicit demand, for it is this one, if it is somewhat developed, that will allow us to detect the contrary demand underlying it. This demand expresses itself as follows: don't lay a finger on my suffering, because it is my unique and fundamental pleasure; I am what I suffer, and thus I could not possibly abandon this suffering without ceasing to exist as I do, and I don't have any other mode of existence available; so curing me of this is obviously out of the question.

Freud made this elementary but decisive discovery in 1892, while using hypnosis to cure a woman who wanted to breast-feed her child but could not. He noticed that there was what he called a counterwill within her, and that, in accordance with the tendency toward hysteria described by Charcot, she was the victim of a dissociation of consciousness. It would be easy to show that it was on the basis of this sort of experience that Freud was able to elaborate his theory of the unconscious, repression, transference, and so on. In other words, it is because Freud wanted to cure that he was able to imagine the fiction of the psychic apparatus; it is because he encountered difficulties in his attempts to cure that he had to invent procedures other than those which hypnotizers had proposed in his day. But he continued to move in the same direction.

Indeed, how can we as contemporary psychoanalysts cure a patient of the refusal to be cured? Or, to return to the vocabulary I was using earlier, how can we detach a person from his unique mode of suffering, from the mode of suffering that is unique to him? For it is this problem that confronts us. The answer to this question is simple and has not varied, not just since the earliest beginnings of Freud's work but probably since Mesmer—indeed, since centuries before him: one cures a patient of the refusal to be cured through hypnosis.

It is becoming less and less comprehensible to me why psychoanalysts make such an outcry when the word *hypnosis* is pronounced, why they arm themselves with ridiculous defenses and repeat in one voice the same magic words, when all I am suggesting is that we simply understand a bit better what it is that we are doing, and to that end, reconnect it with a very old tradition. After all, hypnosis is something basic and everyday that can be quite simply defined as a mixture of distraction and attention.

There is, of course, on one extreme, spectacular hypnosis, in which someone is (for example) put to sleep while undergoing a painless surgical operation; on the other extreme is collective hypnosis, through which a leader or savior can get anything and everything out of a crowd. But between the two extremes exist phenomena of intense attention that distract us from the entire environment, or inversely, phenomena of distraction that allow us to feel and perceive all sorts of facts that escape the most perfect mental concentration—in other words, that allow us to be attentive to them. Distraction and attention are thus two permanently interchangeable phenomena. We may say that we are under hypnosis because we are hyperattentive to a single thing, but also that we are under hypnosis because we have allowed a part of ourselves to go dormant, such that this part enters into a system of communication that does not arise from rational intelligence.

It is this elementary phenomenon that we use in psychoanalysis with the aim of curing a patient of the refusal to be cured. But that final aspect is still off in the distance at the outset of an analysis. The initial task is to distract the patient from what he has come explicitly to demand, and draw his attention toward what he has come implicitly to demand and what he is trying hard not to consider. Take, for example, a patient visiting an analyst for the first time. The patient sits down; the psychoanalyst sits down too and waits. This expectation (Freud uses this word to define hypnosis, then anxiety, and then transference), indeterminate in terms of its length and object, creates a state of panic, confusion, and anxiety in the patient that he does not know how to overcome. All of his attention is directed toward the analyst, but that attention does not help him in any way, because the analyst, for his part, is expecting anything and everything. The patient is then, through this attention, distracted from all of his customary reference points; he lets them go dormant, and his speech, which had been aimed at a communication, breaks down because he is no longer capable of giving it an intentional course, such that he un-speaks. And it is then his anxiety that becomes the guide of his speech, his anxiety that is, precisely, that suffering to which he is attached and which belongs to him uniquely.

This description makes no claims to universality, for things do not always proceed this way. There are obsessional patients who have rehearsed their words, there are hysterical patients who display their suffering or show that it is altogether tolerable, there are perverse patients who know how to be delirious without losing their footing, and so on. In my opinion, however, the preceding description suggests something that every psychoanalyst hopes to see appear as early as possible in analysis: a speech that is no longer under the control of conscious activity and that is thereby very close to the affects constituting the analysand's own unique life. Hypnosis has then shown its dual effect of fixation and de-linking. Because the analysand's attention is fixed on the analyst, whose expectation is indeterminate, the need to fill this void produces the de-linking of a speech that is looking everywhere and nowhere for an object where the analysand's anxiety can settle.

Does that mean that one has thereby obtained some measure of a cure for the refusal to be cured? No; what occurs is instead the opposite: the refusal to be cured is fully displayed, in the form of transference neurosis. Just as mass panic ends only through submission to a savior-figure, the analysand's astute anxiety subsides in the analyst's confident or trustful expectation (another term Freud used to designate hypnosis and transference). What does that mean? It means that the analysand can now give free expression to this refusal to be cured, which is both his mode of suffering and his mode of existence, or more precisely in this case his mode of relating to others, his own way of living the relationship of alterity.

Transference neurosis reproduces neurosis inasmuch as the latter can be reduced to a particular, always identical way of situating oneself in relation to others. For example, take the case of a woman whose only way of surviving in the presence of a mother who was negative and perceived as threatening was through a masochistic retreat in which she reveled in the void, by making herself a void or creating one around her. The analyst's silence is then used to rediscover that position. If the analyst appears unwavering or exasperated, that gives the analysand one more reason to retreat into her void; but if the analyst seems to understand, the analysand regards that as an even greater threat, a way of forcing open the empty space that is the refuge for her minimal existence. In both cases, the transference neurosis is reinforced and hypnosis no longer plays its contradictory role of fixation and de-linking, or rather, the two terms are indissolubly fused together: the process of undoing the connection between the void and self-destruction is constantly fed and revived by the fixation on the menacing Other. We are well aware that situations of this sort are not chimerical and that numerous analyses get bogged down in them.

Sometimes, the mortally constrained quality of such a situation is resolved by turning to another analyst. Why? It is undoubtedly because, thanks to the work that has already been done, this other analyst can immediately perceive what has happened and succeeds in keeping himself from getting stuck in the dilemma in which the analysand's attitude is, "if you stay silent, you're a torturer, and if you understand, you're even worse, because you're torturing me in my very interiority." Obviously, resorting to another analyst should not be necessary; it should be possible to modify one's position such that the primary hypnosis of the first sessions is broken and the patient is forced to focus his attention on another point so that his neurotic mechanism can be thrown out of order once again. (This entails passing from one hypnosis to another.)

For example, it is enough in some cases for the psychoanalyst to admit, because he really thinks so, that he is incapable of pursuing the analysis, for the entire hypnotic edifice to collapse—that is, for the analysand to stop pursuing any further his trustful expectation. Or, to give another example, it is enough for the analyst to become aware, after months or even years, of the exact, very precise, very particular position in which he has been placed by the analysand, and to refuse within himself to stay in that position, in order for transference neurosis to cease to be possible—that is, for the two attached faces of hypnosis to become detached. In this case, the analysand is brutally returned to himself: he perceives that it is he, aided by the analyst, who has fabricated this scene in order to be able to reproduce what is closest to his heart—namely, his manner of suffering through others, of suffering permanently with the help of a fantasized relationship to others.

These examples simply indicate something far more radical: the end of transference neurosis can take place only if the analyst loses his position, no longer holds his position, and no longer serves to uphold the typical relationship reproduced in the analysis by the patient. What happened? How is it possible for this to happen?

If, through his displacement, the psychoanalyst is no longer the support for the neurotic relationship that is reproduced in transference, the analysand will not fail to be anxious about this. But, at the heart of that anxiety, he knows that the psychoanalyst is still there, that he is in a certain way far more present than he was earlier. In fact, he is present as someone who trusts, who has recognized in the person of the analysand a possibility for displacing himself, too, and for freeing himself from the bonds of his neurosis. The psychoanalyst is then in the position of a father (or mother) who knows that he can no longer do anything for his child, and is certain through his attentive proximity that he will under no circumstances be obliged to fill in for that child in taking charge of his destiny. The analyst is, in this case, present through the respect that pushes the other party to move forward at his own risk, a respect that does indeed provoke in the analysand the necessity of respecting himself by ceasing to feel incapable of moving or nourishing himself, of marching forward in his life and undertaking to invent it. He is the sole origin of this personal life, and no one can make him take charge of himself and depend on himself. The temptation to complain has just been removed from the analysand, as has the temptation to blame his woes on his parents, his nanny, his grandmother, or his little brother. He is henceforth alone in the world, facing life.

If he overcomes this ordeal his anxiety, rather than submerging him, subsides. For anxiety is always the index of a decision that has not been made in time and to which one must now resort. Anxiety—that internal tumult that arises from the absence of reference points, that tempest of things and beings that collide in the vain quest to find their place, that panic in the face of the excessive complexity of the real which one must, in spite of everything, confront—evaporates like clouds lifting with the breeze. The decision to carry the weight of one's existence, and to entrust no one else with taking care of it, has the effect of reshuffling the cards the analysand had been holding but had refused to use up to that point.

But what can this saving decision rely upon in order to be accomplished? There must certainly be a force that was previously unknown and that can now have its chance to act. What has happened is that hypnosis, properly understood, has come into play. Transference reproduced in suffering a certain type of relationship, and it was forbidden to abandon this suffering because it was intrinsically connected to relationships to which the analysand was accustomed—indeed, to relationships that constituted him in the only painful singularity he knew. How can he change, that is, pass from one type of relationship to another in which his suffering would no longer be indispensable to him? He can do so quite simply through the change carried out by the analyst, who has stopped playing the game of the neurotic relationship and established another one. The psychoanalyst has not made himself absent, he has not abandoned his interlocutor. Rather he has shown him, after a long approach, that it is possible to remain in solitude and that solitude implies that one is tied to others who are solitary, too.

But what does hypnosis have to do with any of that? To put it differently, of what is this solitude made? Moreover, where is this new force hiding, and how can it come to light? Concentration, which is perhaps simply another name for hypnosis, is this descent to the source. It rids one of all preoccupations, of all cares, and even of all thoughts and feelings; it excludes the particular forms of objects that are the lot of our daily attention; and it stops at nothing determined in order to bring about an expectation that goes in all directions. In short, it gives us access to life in and of itself. One might be able to say of a desperate man that he has loved everything about life and in life, but that he has not loved life. He was able to distract himself with everything that offers avid youth the dazzle of things discovered and to become intoxicated with the speed of his journey; but he could not take the time to pause and run the risk of being understood. Loving life, before it burgeons or below its burgeoning point, requires a process of stripping down and, in a sense, abstracting all of the figures life can assume. Loving life means dredging the well of our existence that the torments of the desert have obstructed, so that the necessary water is able to flow once again.

The analyst who embraces his solitude in order to provoke that of the analysand has arrived at this point. He is expecting: that is, he is in a state of extreme attention, with all of his senses sharpened, yet without wanting or desiring anything, in a state of suspense ready for whatever may arise. He is, by that very fact, at the peak of the force that is facing him, of the force that has presented itself and that cannot help transmitting to the analysand the attraction, the seduction, and the draw of the same force within himself. Thus, there is no room left for a discourse seeking a meaning that slips away through its insufficiency, that slips through his fingers because he never grasps anything of reality beyond its surface layer. The need to tell one's story is exhausted.

At the end of an analysis, only one expression is left that can say everything and nothing, that expresses the completion of that which is beginning, that translates, not the plenitude of a leaf but the irrepressible vigor of a seed, "I am living." This obvious fact contains within itself the possibility of all renewals, the capacity for receiving from the same source everything that events will bring later: the courage to face obstacles or adversity. The fact that we are truly able to pronounce this simple expression supposes that we have moved past the dispersion triggered by the diversity of our daily acts and conversely, that for a moment at least, we have allowed a primary energy to accumulate; we have no longer given that energy the opportunity to expend itself. The exercise of concentration that has cleared the ground of our concerns has produced the concentration of force. In our attempts at explanation, interpretation, and meaning, we no longer feel inclined to expend that force.

It is no longer a matter of talking in order to give a meaning to the symptoms unveiled by transference neurosis and, through that, of gathering them into the net of the rational. It is no longer a matter of seeking to determine "why your daughter is mute"; what matters now is figuring out how to restore her hearing. For that, one must undergo once again the living being's most fundamental experience, the one that can, in the case of a human being, lead him to the very heart of the principle that organizes his existence in the world. An animal, especially when it has never had any contact with humans, is always spontaneously in agreement with its organism and its environment; it is always immersed in its body and in its milieu, always adapted in relation to its own possibilities. It is our privilege to be able to place ourselves at a distance from our own functioning and thus, for better or worse, to disrupt the immediacy of this immersion. We are in the world after our fashion because we cannot do otherwise. To be cured, one must and one need only plunge into that experience once again. Putting an end to transference neurosis presupposes putting an end to the analysis, which signifies that putting an end to transference neurosis implies experiencing the discovery of life's organizing sense, insofar as concentration permits such a discovery. In other words, putting an end to transference neurosis means turning back, turning away from the effort to represent oneself, in order to turn toward life at a level below that at which it becomes manifestly complex.

Would the ideal, then, be to become animals? No, not in any case. Biology has already taught us that, through his uncontested superiority among creatures endowed with a brain, the human being never ceases to remake himself, for his development continues right up until his death. Ethology likewise underscores that animals are incapable of eventually overcoming the handicaps and traumas of their birth or earliest days. We are thus not suggesting that human beings should revert to a state of blissful animality. The human being is capable of analyzing his deficiencies and his malformations. Let us say that, thanks to neurosis transference, he is capable of uncovering everything that is not going well. After that, however, he must not pursue this undertaking beyond what is necessary. He must take the opposite direction and go, through concentration, to the place where this unique power of redeployment will fully play its role and reveal its effects.

A man who has undergone this experience said he wanted to shout to the world how easy it was. For months he had expressed the uncontrollable need of a hypochondriacal anxiety. Every time he tried to concentrate, this anxiety would fill his head with cutting remarks that kept him from changing: "Go ahead and talk, you know very well that you'll never get by without me." After a crisis that he had found particularly painful and that made him doubt the trust he had placed in the analyst, he had decided to trust in himself, to overcome his fears and risk confronting this anxiety.

It had occurred to him that his life could be reduced to that of a plant; he had become, for a time, a vigorous herb, well rooted in the soil, and right next to the freshness of a stream he had known during his childhood. He had then been able to approach without fear the unknown horror of his mother's body. Thus, from that day when, in a state of concentration, he had identified with the most elementary life, he had abandoned his need for anxiety. He was astonished at how simple it was, but with enough peace and certainty that he was not inclined to bother with extra justifications.

How does one free onself from the need for suffering, and what does suffering then become? One suffers, as we said earlier, in order to preserve a neurotic mode of relation. Yet one also suffers in order to give oneself the sensation of existing. When a person's sensorial, perceptive, affective, and intellectual system gives him no cause for concern over its functioning, the living thing that we are is designed in such a way that he forgets to be astonished at existing and to perceive that he exists. He will then go to those around him and ask them to make him suffer, or he will make himself suffer when he comes into contact with them, in order to avoid the solitude that would be the other means—this one far more risky—of knowing that he is alive. Yet, given that this solitude remains on the horizon, we will have to pass through suffering once again, as through a necessary step. Suffering is like the dead leaves that fall from the trees and decay in order to turn into fertile loam, that rich and friable soil where future living things will grow. "A person who hasn't suffered, what does he know?" But the person who does not remain attached to his suffering undergoes the refined experience of the variety of modes of existence; he accedes to the hypersensitivity of all forms of the living.

If hypnosis is the concentration of life and on life, it no longer has anything to do with the mere fascination through which it is ordinarily defined. It is already, deep within, the development of life outside. It is prolonged through self-hypnosis, both that of the analysand and that of the analyst, whose solitudes create the capacity for greater self-revelation. Transference neurosis comes to an end because the analysis comes to an end; and the analysis comes to an end because life takes on a new intensity.

We will have to go a bit further still: since the pursuit of analysis is an imperative, the best way to get there is to become an analyst. The analyst has the same goal, for he has already gone in the direction of representation, which is his major concern, and will thus seek to represent himself in and through disciples, and the best way to do that (I'm going quickly because all of this is well known) is for his disciples to gather at a single institution. Moreover, there's no need to force them into it, since transference neurosis continues to be effective. And, in the event that transference threatens to weaken, one can invent the transference of work.

I could obviously go on at length in this direction. It would be easy to show that all of this has its internal coherence and derives from the premisses with which we began. If analysis has no limit in time and space, transference neurosis will tend to invade everything; the analysis will not only last as long as life does, it will absorb all of life. And the outside world will disappear. One may even dream of creating a new type of social bond, through psychoanalysis.

Chapter 11

In Certain Cases

It is, undoubtedly, bold on my part to come before such an audience [the medical staff of the Maison Blanche Hospital] to speak about transference in psychosis. For it is clear that, as a result of your daily practice, you know far more about this subject than I do. I only hope I can succeed in raising a few questions that we can then discuss together.

Is it, first of all, legitimate to speak of a possible treatment for psychoses, when one hasn't specified what one is talking about? You already know how difficult it is to make diagnoses and how multiform the illness is in certain cases. What's more, you see people arriving in the hospital or in your office who one might classify in the same psychiatric rubric yet who are nonetheless quite different. Even if, for example, they both present traits characteristic of psychosis, what a distance there is in prognosis between a seventeen-year-old boy or girl and a person whose affliction is chronic, between a deeply disturbed child and one who is autistic!

But that still does not suffice to show the complexity of the therapeutic problems that confront us. For example, it is not the lesser degree of seriousness in a psychosis that can lead us to make a favorable prognosis. In certain mild cases, the impossibility of establishing a relationship rules out any perspective for a cure; whereas conversely in certain very serious cases, hope is permitted because the doctor has been able to establish a relationship with the patient in question. To give another example, it sometimes happens that schizophrenics, when they are hospitalized, do not refrain from undergoing therapy, even a psychoanalysis; conversely, certain schizophrenics, still socialized, shut themselves off in a state of total affective indifference. The reason for this is that an effective or possibly effective therapy would risk shattering the defenses that allow them to remain in their workplace. It is because they stay insensitive, or indifferent, that they are able to maintain the minimum level of interaction with others that is required by society. Therefore, we are faced with an infinite variety of situations, and only detailed analyses of numerous cases can teach us something about the criteria for a possible therapy for psychotics.

I have used the expression "in certain cases." These are also the words I've chosen for the title of this essay. The first reason is that I meet a certain number of psychiatrists who are discouraged deep down because they would like to be able to improve the state of everyone with whom they rub shoulders. The second reason is that if you try to put all psychoses in the same basket, to trace them all back to the same cause under a single theoretical formula, you end up no longer understanding anything.

Let me begin by talking a bit about transference. The word was originally used by Freud to explain, in the case of neurosis, how an affect that should have been tied to a representation was separated from it, and transferred to another representation which did not have an intrinsic link with this affect and in which the affect could not, therefore, express itself. The goal of therapy was then to reestablish the connection between the affect and the representation suited to it.

This first definition of transference has some importance. For, when Freud discovered transference in the analytic cure, he used the word in the plural for a long time. For him, it was a question of discerning transferences: that is, the traits of the analyst that were used by patients to represent a given symptomatic trait. Freud thought that he could thereby overcome the neurosis by undoing it, transference after transference. I emphasize this point because it strikes me as crucial in analysis to move from the singular to the plural. I will return to that in a moment.

Later, Freud spoke about transference in the singular to refer to the powerful affective bond through which a patient is attached to the analyst. He repeatedly said that this bond was the mainspring of the cure, and that this mainspring was the same in nature as that which he had seen at work in hypnosis. But he also noted that this bond reproduced the neurosis and was then quite difficult to break.

It is, I think, in this context that we should understand his declaration that psychotics are incapable of transferring. There are, without any doubt, several possible explanations for this theoretical stance. I will dwell on only one of them: psychotics are incapable of transference because the transference they make onto the doctor or psychoanalyst is not manageable. And it is not manageable because it does not respect the structure, properly speaking, of transference. The psychiatrist or psychoanalyst who is the object of transference is not fantasized by the patient because this psychotic patient is incapable of forming phantasms, in the sense that he would be incapable of distinguishing between a phantasm and a delirium or hallucination, because he believes in his delirium or hallucination; he takes them for realities. Now, in psychoanalysis, phantasms must be worked through as such and not taken for realities of the outside world.

We will return to that idea, but it seems to me that one could formulate the reverse hypothesis and defend it just as well: psychotics are especially apt at transference, or rather psychotics reveal to us what is the very essence of transference. In what sense? What I see as the basis of transference in the psychotic is the impossibility of making a distinction between himself and the other. For him, there is no *two*: either he is absorbed by the other, or he absorbs the other. He has the other in him and it devours him, or conversely, he devours the other. There is only enough life for one. It is he or I, it is she or I. In other words, it is either alienation through the other, who manipulates him and forbids him from attaining any sort of autonomy, or it is separation, pure and simple, from the other. We often hear remarks of this sort: "If I separate myself from my mother, she will die, because she lives through me, she stays alive through me"; and, on the other hand, "If I don't separate myself from my mother (although sometimes it's the father) I'm going to die, because I don't have any life of my own."

Yet might it not be true that this extreme position adopted by the psychotic shows us something that is present in every human relationship and, in a very visible manner, in passion? In the case of a violent love, which we can all experience, there is not any room for two either. It's the lover's refrain: I can't live without you, I die if you go away from me, but having you near makes me merge into you and disappear. A character in a Truffaut film says, "I can't be without you or with you"—a double bond that leads to homicide and suicide. This has led some to say that love is hate. There is, indeed, no difference when this paroxysm has been reached between life and death. Life is death. We are indeed at the border of psychosis here, and passion is rightly called a madness. If we listen to neurotics in analysis, we end up hearing the same thing in certain cases. This is particularly striking in mother-daughter relations; the games of identification are sometimes a life-and-death matter. And we also find this in certain cases of feminine homosexuality.

What I would like to suggest is that there is no solution of continuity between neurosis and psychosis. In an analysis that has been pursued far enough, in certain cases, or always, one has the sense of touching a sort of psychotic core at the heart of the individual undergoing analysis. A mixture of rejection and fusion, this psychotic core is very difficult to overcome, given that the very heart of psychic life is so closely tied to this pleasure [*jouissance*], and abandoning it or turning one's back to it gives the analysand the impression that he is going to lose the best part of himself. In a sense, this is exactly what allows him to subsist.

We thus find ourselves grappling with a singular paradox: What prevents us from living, this point of madness, is at the same time the thing to which we are most attached as a means of continuing to live. Yet this is a paradox that can be understood because it reproduces the paradox of every human relationship, where distance is often inadequate since the other is too near or too far. Life and death, love and hate, the relationship is a nonrelationship.

This is not meant to erase the difference between psychosis and neurosis. In the case of psychosis, the relationship to the other is defined by an alternation of alienation and separation: the other is the person who invades me or the person for whom I am nothing. In the case of neurosis, we can suppose an intertwining of alterity and appropriation: the other counts for me as an other because he is different, but the other is also the person who makes me live and who authorizes me to appropriate him for myself. Or, to phrase it differently, I have something uniquely mine that he recognizes he doesn't have and is not, and I let him take me and leave me, take some of this from me and leave it to me.

We can, however, go further in our description of the so-called transferential relationship. If, in psychosis, there are two subjects and there cannot be two, in neurosis, and especially in analysis, there are four and there have to be four.

First of all, in the most banal manner, we could say that there is never any dual relationship in psychoanalysis (but that is undoubtedly true of any human relationship), given that every individual is divided between a consciousness and an unconscious. But this remark doesn't take us very far, for we would have to suppose four subjects, two consciousnesses, and two unconsciouses. And it is not clear that the expression *subject* is pertinent for signifying the unity of consciousness, much less of the unconscious.

Rather, I would like to describe things such as they are presented in our experience, or at least such as we can imagine them on the basis of the thinking habits of our mini-culture. In a cure of a neurotic patient, our task at the start of the analysis is to teach the patient to associate; in other words, we introduce him onto the other scene, to use Freud's vocabulary. Associating without reserve entails leaving the regimen of speech imposed by society to accede to that which I called elsewhere un-speech. This un-speech, which is not ruled by the necessities of communication, uncovers the phantasms, the imaginings, the desires that govern our entire life and that are not subjected to the reality principle, that challenge the reality of the outside world and of life in society. It is still something of ourselves that is revealed in this manner, but that cannot be revealed outside of the analyst's office. The patient is thus two: he is this social persona with all of its masks and all of its illusions, and he is also this secret other who directs all of the moves in the comedy. He is this particular person, and he is this patient as well, to the extent that he really functions as an analysand.

The analyst, in turn, is two: he or she is this man or woman with his or her particularities, limits, prejudices, emotions and thoughts, but he or she is also a function that does not have a name, an x on whom the patient will be able to fantasize as he pleases, whom he will take for his father or mother, for his brother, sister, or friend, on whom he will bestow omnipotence or powerlessness, and thanks to whom he will be able to become double. The analyst is therefore two: he or she is the person of the analyst, and also the function of analyst. It is important that, in the cure itself, this duality on the part of the analyst be present. What I mean is that it is not enough to note the fact that a given psychoanalyst has a social life and is, on top of that, a psychoanalyst. It is as an analyst that his division must be accomplished; it is as an analyst that he is simultaneously a pure function without individuality, and a person who is there with his thoughts, his phantasms, and his reactions.

It is sometimes difficult, particularly at the beginning of an analysis, to set these four terms in place. The analyst must draw upon his art so that the patient does not get bogged down in recounting the adventures of his present or past existence, but rather feels that he is an other as well, an other who surprises him through dreams, slips of the tongue, and strange behaviors. It often happens that the analysis does not take place, because it unfolds through an excess of reality and an absence of imagination or of phantasm.

You are quite familiar with all of this. I am taking the liberty of lingering on these obvious facts because they allow us to describe conversely what happens for the psychotic. For example, in the case of a delirious patient we suffer, in our relationship with him, from an excess of imagination, for reality is totally absorbed in stories, evocations, or silences in the sense that we no longer have any means of intervening.

If, in the case of a neurotic patient, we have a great deal of difficulty in making the other scene appear, in the case of the psychotic we find it hard to establish any distance at all in regard to that which is imposed upon the patient. In his case, therefore, we must work backward in a sense: that is, we must begin by entering into delirium and hallucination.

I recall that one day at the Hospital of Sainte-Anne, when I was just starting out, the chief physician had asked me to see a patient. The case involved a young man who didn't seem to have any serious symptoms and who spoke in a manner that seemed very coherent. He talked to me about his parents; his father, he said, was German, and his mother Austrian. I murmured to him, "That's sort of the same culture." He interrupted me sharply: "No, they have absolutely nothing to do with each other." A while later, he told me about his school, where he liked only his Russian teacher and his gym teacher. I was the one who then said that they had nothing to do with each other. The conversation continued in the same vein. He always connected things that, in his words, had nothing to do with each other. After an hour I left him and went to tell the chief physician that this boy must be a schizophrenic who could be dangerous. She smiled, because she didn't believe a word of it. But the next day the patient ran away and came back to the hospital with an awl thirty centimeters long, and then a bottle of sulfuric acid was found in his suitcase. He wanted simply to warn us about his dangerous character and be placed in a secured ward. I didn't cure him, and never even saw him again. But I drew a lesson from this incident: if we want to understand anything about a person's way of speaking, even if it doesn't have the flowing appearance of a delirium, we have to begin by entering into it.

Entering into a person's delirium means raving along with him, that is, showing enough imagination to give the delirium the resonances we are capable of giving it. It means, in a sense, participating in a delirium *à deux*, even as we maintain a certain distance to control it. What then happens is something quite unique: on the one hand, the analyst's involvement splits in two, between the function which remains intact and the work of imagination in which he engages; on the other hand, the patient too will split in two, for he will know which of our comments to take and which to leave. We come to exist for him to the extent that he will accept what suits him out of the amplification we give to his delirium, but also to the extent that he will become capable of rejecting what does not suit him. When we enter into the delirium of a psychotic in this manner, we have at least a fifty percent chance of being wrong, and he will be delighted to take us for an imbecile who doesn't understand anything, even though he knows that we understand sometimes. With a psychotic, at least in the cases where he speaks, we cannot avoid speaking and thus running the constant risk that we will utter stupidities. But it is on this basis that he will be able to assert his autonomy, and if he explicitly asserts this autonomy of his delirium before another and for another, a big step has been taken. For he has then emerged out of the solitary assertion that traps him in his madness.

So perhaps what happens with him is not so far removed from what can happen with a neurotic. Without a doubt, prolonged silence is indispensable for making the other scene appear. Speaking too much runs the risk of transforming the cure into a conversation that conforms to the rules of all life in society, but not speaking does not give the analysand the hold over our words and our person that could allow him to distinguish himself and not remain in a fantasized relationship with us. We are well aware that errors in interpretation are just as precious in analysis as are correct formulations. It is our errors that can knock us down from our omnipotence, an omnipotence which the analysand wants to maintain at any price so that he will not have to fall out of his own. That is why it often happens that an analysand makes his analyst shut up, under the pretext that he is saying stupidities, but in reality because this analysand wants to trap the analyst in his function, with the aim of reestablishing the dual relationship that saves him from splitting in two himself.

While treating psychotics in my office, I have on occasion had a similar sort of experience concerning fear. In certain cases, what is hidden by an incoherent manner of speaking is violence, the violence of which the patient feels capable and which can go as far as the wish or possibility of killing. For this violence to have a chance to be spoken, the analysand must transmit a feeling of fear to the analyst or the therapist (whichever term you prefer). Indeed, what the patient wants, to be sure that his fear has been perceived, is to make us feel it in turn. But if we want to have a chance of establishing a change, it is necessary for us to undergo a split that follows the distinction I proposed earlier between the function and the person. If we confine ourselves to pure function and settle for perceiving the fear of the other from the outside, his fear will rage until the moment when he eventually makes us feel it through gestures of violence. If, to the contrary, we are simply a person who is afraid, in certain cases the patient will repress his fear and protect us, because he wants to remain in a relationship with us. Whether we stick simply to our function or allow ourselves only to feel, nothing truly happens in the patient, who remains in the same relationship to his fear. There is then only a relation between two terms, in the form of a brutal shock or isolation.

What we must subtly succeed in doing is to accept feeling the fear as a person while also taking a distance from it through our function. We are afraid, but we accept this fear for what it is in the therapeutic relationship, a game through which the patient tells us that his violence is not a force that he could use to act and produce, but that it is not aimed at destroying the other person in the relationship. If we achieve this split between the reality of the fear and the game of making the other person afraid then what results, in certain cases, is that the patient enters into the game and perceives that he wanted to make us afraid in order to rid himself of his own fear.

I don't think that we are very far in this instance from what happens, in many cases, in analysis. From the earliest sessions, the analysand tries to measure not the analyst's degree of intelligence or competence, or whether he has nice eyes and a well- or poorly cut suit, but rather his degree of resistance to the violence of speech. He wonders quite simply if the analyst will be able to bear what he himself cannot bear, a certain pressure he does not control, a force that unsettles him, a cruelty he inflicts on himself. Especially in the early days of my practice, I was astonished that patients took so many sessions to say at last why they had come. What they fear is that they will blurt out something that will come back and hit them right in the face or in the heart because the analyst, incapable of taking it on and bearing it, will throw it back at them. It is hasty, far too hasty, to tell the analysand to say everything that pops into his head when we are not capable of hearing it.

But it is not a question of hiding behind our armor, either— that is, of confining ourselves to function; for when you are sure you understand everything you understand nothing. The speech of the other person must indeed reach us, but at the same time what reaches us must not destabilize us, or at least not for too long. Otherwise, like the psychotic, in certain cases the neurotic will try to protect us from his words. He will come back faithfully, but to say nothing, because he will be afraid of disturbing us.

I have occasionally seen some of my analysands leave without telling me why they had left. Some of them came back a year or two later, and the first thing one or two of them told me was, "I came to see if you had changed." In other words, they were wondering: Am I finally going to be able to speak without fear of hurting you and of seeing the blow I've inflicted come back to me like a boomerang? But conversely, in other cases, I have sometimes heard the rage of analysands reproaching me for bearing anything, for letting myself be crushed by them without reacting—in short, for sinking into the masochism so dear to certain analysts. Perhaps, at such moments, I was confining myself to my function and was incapable of metabolizing their words in order to send them back to them in a distanced interpretation. Instead of a game with four terms, there were, once again, only two left.

Of course, it is all far more complex than this description allows me to convey. For example, the function of the analyst is an undetermined x, an other without singularity in the relationship. But this indetermination allows the analysand to turn the analyst into whatever he wishes: the analyst can be his father, his mother, his brother, his sister, or any other person he pleases, in the form that pleases him. Now, it is critically important that the analyst perceive the position that has been assigned to him, which is not so easy. This can be seen quite clearly when an analyst is being observed by a supervisor. It often becomes obvious to the supervising analyst who is listening to an analyst as he speaks to an analysand that this analyst holds a given, determined place—for example, that he is a character subjected to hate or who must be protected from hate, that he is the refuge in the case of abandonment or, to the contrary, the person whom the analysand provokes to abandon him in order to return to an infantile situation.

What is very curious is that the analyst being observed does not need, once he has perceived where he has been placed, to say to his analysand where the latter is placing him. It is enough for him to know and accept this position, for the analysand to talk about it and modify the relationship. In that sense we do not work solely with language but, in some instances, without saying anything, by adopting the position that the analysand wants to assign us.

This place spotted by the analyst sometimes designates the fundamental form of relationship that the analysand repeats in every situation. But the fact that the analyst recognizes this place obliges the analysand to invent a new type of relationship. One could define the cure as the possibility, through transference, of ceasing to repeat a single and stereotypical form of relationship in order to learn new forms whose number is infinite. I said at the outset that the success of a cure can be defined as the passage from the singular to the plural. Here is one way of bringing about that passage, the future plural for the analysand being the corollary of the possibility for the analyst to place himself in various positions. We analysts must be able to be a father, a mother, a sister, a brother, a friend, but also an animal, a tree, a rock. In short, we must be able to return to the diversity of all the individualities in nature after having taken ourselves to be a psychoanalyst, or, perhaps, passed ourselves off as one.

To conclude, I would like to tell you the simple—and thus dangerous—idea that underlies everything I've written or, at least, that saves me from getting lost in a pure description that has no beginning and no end: we reproduce in transference the quintessence of our way of being in relation—not, of course, our way of being visibly in relation in social life, but the fundamental way in which we place the other, in other words our strictly personal or singular way of hating and loving, of killing or allowing to live, of exploiting and of sacrificing ourselves. Just as planets are situated at a certain distance from each other in function of their mass so, too, each of us, in function of our weight or our futility, is located at a fixed distance from everyone else.

Transference reproduces this fundamental manner of being; and just as one speaks in painting of fundamental color, it is up to us to discover the harmonious colors, for an individual can reveal, if we listen to him, a complexity and variants that we will have to set into play in order to modify the monolithic quality of the fundamental relationship that arises from neurosis. Partializing, "pluralizing," to use a neologism—that is, discovering and making the analyst discover that he is many people—will be the task of the cure; this will be the surest means of relativizing, which is the surest means of finding reality once more. We will then be able to invoke Anna de Noailles's expression: "Our heart is innumerable." The plurality of our phantasms will refer back with a bit more flexibility to the plurality of reality.

Chapter 12

The Cure

It seems that the entire history of psychotherapy during the scientific era has been marked by concern over the cure. I am using the term *psychotherapy* even though it dates from the end of the nineteenth century, whereas its history begins with the last quarter of the eighteenth century. There is not, however, any single word that can be applied to all of that history.

Is it true that psychoanalysis marks a decisive break in this field, and if so, how can we characterize that break? That will be my first question. If psychoanalysis operates through transference, that is, through transference neurosis, how is it possible that it liberates the patient from this neurosis? That will be my second question. And if the answer turns out to be negative, what can we propose to put an end to transference, or what meaning can we give to transference so that we can claim to put an end to it? That will be my third question.

If we trace the history of psychotherapy's attempt to exist in the face of (or, rather, thanks to) science back to Franz-Anton Mesmer's arrival in France, we can say that it is essentially directed, first and foremost, at curing. Crises would have had no interest for Mesmer if he could not use them to justify the curative effects of his magnetic fluid. But, as he said himself, and as Lavoisier pointed out after being appointed to the government commission charged with determining whether magnetism was real, the cure doesn't prove anything, because one never knows whether nature (in the sense that word held at the end of the eighteenth century) would not have cured the ailments of Mesmer's patients without the use of this supposedly effective means. Obviously these comments were made before the era of scientific medicine, but they are still valuable for psychotherapies. For the means cannot be isolated, and one can never test them by applying the differential method set forth by John Stuart Mill; it is for that reason that the question of curing is not easy to raise.

However, while it did not neglect the perspective of curing, the history of mesmerism (also known as animal magnetism) developed in a different direction. Mesmerism was used to acquire internal knowledge of the body and long-distance vision. A multitude of experiments were done that are echoed in literature—as, for example, in Balzac's *Ursule Mirouët*, where animal magnetism plays a very decisive role. For Balzac, as for many others, animal magnetism was considered to be a science that one could verify, a science that, of course, entailed an initiation. It was the soul, the psyche entered into sleep—that is, liberated from the determinations imposed on it by the senses—and unaware of time and space that was free to communicate with everything.

I am not making these historical remarks gratuitously: they show that, in our culture, as soon as one approaches psychotherapy, it is no longer simply a therapy; rather it seeks, in one way or another, to be a science that believes it has access to areas about which the exact and thus objective sciences cannot help knowing nothing. In fact, for Lavoisier the action of animal magnetism had to be explained as an effect of the imagination; for him, the imagination was nothing, since everything that was not materially observable was of no interest. This did not keep Mesmer and certain of his disciples from declaring that they were practicing a science. I will leave aside that story, along with the very complex history of hypnosis, where one could, I believe, also see at work the dual preoccupations with curing and with scientificity. I'll move directly to the subject of psychoanalysis.

Freud's work, too, is thoroughly pervaded by the concern of using psychoanalysis with a view to curing neurosis, but also by the effort to achieve scientific knowledge of a field that was neglected by the sciences of his day. I think that it is futile to give this claim broader justifications, given that they are available to everyone today. What I wish to do is underscore that the cure itself is subjected to this double imperative: of curing and of scientificity. However, we should note right away that this fact is going to complicate considerably our attempt to devise a theoretical explanation of the place that is granted to curing in psychoanalysis.

The same fact complicates the task assigned to the psychoanalyst in practice. It is as if there were a sort of conflict, an opposition between the aim of curing and the scientific aim.

Let us try to define the cure—something that is extremely difficult to do in psychoanalysis. I will borrow a formula, a negative definition of the cure, from Freud's *Introductory Lectures on Psychoanalysis*: "The neurotic is incapable of enjoying and of acting, of enjoying because he is obliged to spend a great deal of energy to maintain his libido in a state of repression and to shield himself from its assaults" (*S.E.*, 16:453–54). We could interpret this sentence as telling us, in general, the effect of symptoms. The cure would, conversely, be defined as the possibility of enjoying and acting at least a bit more or a bit better. We see immediately that the cure in psychoanalysis cannot be understood as a restitution of a former integrity, as is commonly said, but rather as the production of a state that has never been given. But how is the cure obtained?

Knowledge certainly plays a part in the process. The analyst doesn't attack the symptoms directly; one could almost say that he doesn't pay attention to them. He hopes that they will disappear as the thing that had been repressed comes to consciousness or becomes conscious—that is, essentially, through the recollection of the infantile. And it is incontestable that the process of putting the infantile into words, or as Lacan said, verbalization, has beneficial effects. This obvious fact might absolve us from having to linger on this subject. But I am going to linger, because it is the difficulties that are interesting. We know from Freud himself that this position, perfectly in keeping with theory, did not yield the expected success. He was forced to admit that memories are repeated through acts in transference, and as a solution, he had to propose another form of abreaction in the guise of perlaboration (as he himself put it). Perlaboration is a decisive term, the culmination of the cure, but Freud hardly elaborated on it at all. Repeating or perlaborating no longer means becoming conscious, much less knowing. For the cure to be achieved, wouldn't it therefore be necessary for knowledge and the attempt at knowledge to be unsuccessful? We must conclude that the initiation into the mysteries of the unconscious, however extensive it may be, is not in itself capable of curing. There may thus be a certain conflict that we should register between the two concerns of psychoanalysis: that of curing and that of knowing.

Perhaps, before taking up the second question I proposed, I can give an example of the conflict created by the position of the analysis that is oriented toward knowing. Much has been said about transference-love, but it may not have been sufficiently noted that transference-love appears quite particularly when the psychoanalyst settles for seeking to know, and avoids entering into a relationship in order to play out the abstraction and the artifice of his phantasmatic role on the scene of transference. Through the analyst's will to know, analysands are thus transformed into objects of knowledge or of science; but, because this situation is unbearable for them, they try to lead the analyst onto the scene of reality. Wanting to know, instead of participating in a game that is undoubtedly by turns a comedy, by turns a tragedy, also provokes the analysand to leave the field of play and artifice in order to seek out the realization of his or her phantasms. We know that hysterics are masters at this; they know how to make the analyst fall into the double trap of the taste for knowledge and the exaltation of love.

If psychoanalysis has made a break with the psychic therapies that preceded it, we should, in my opinion, look for that break not in an opposition between knowing and curing, but rather in an expanded definition of knowledge and in the elaboration of a theory whose richness is unmatched. Yet transference poses a problem precisely for this knowledge that seeks to be scientific. We know that Freud never constructed a theory of transference, in contrast to what he did for dreams, jokes, or slips of the tongue. What he transmitted to us was not an excess of knowledge, but not enough. And psychoanalysis is still undoubtedly plagued by this problem. These observations will be extremely valuable for grasping the answer that I will propose to the third question.

We must first, however, raise the second question. If psychoanalysis works through transference and is identified with transference neurosis, how can it cure someone of this neurosis through the same process of transference? We have no difficulty in granting that neurosis can be cured through transference neurosis, just as certain diseases are cured by being inoculated at minimal doses, although the harmful effects of the inoculated disease must disappear after a while so that it can be simply integrated into the organism in the form of a defense system. If I ask, "How can we cure someone of transference neurosis through transference neurosis?" I find myself in a situation just as absurd as if I had asserted, "One must cure someone of a vaccination through a vaccination."

The classic answer is that to overcome this provoked neurosis, transference must be dissolved. But isn't it then analysis itself that will have to end since, without transference, there can be no analysis? Freud never really found a way out of this dilemma. In fact, he advanced ideas on the subject of transference that seem rather contradictory.

Take, for example, his first idea: sometimes Freud considers transference to be a powerful instrument that allows the analyst to act for the good of the patient, and sometimes he says it plays into the hands of resistance. Or, to cite another idea: sometimes he presents transference as an artifact that should be used only temporarily, and sometimes, to the contrary, he describes its resolution or its disappearance as being so difficult as to be impossible. It is as if psychoanalysis had discovered a marvelous remedy that it was then incapable of doing without. One illness was replaced with another illness that couldn't be cured. We must, therefore, rephrase the question in this way: How is it possible to cure someone of transference neurosis?

Before trying to answer that, I would like to consider the expression *transference neurosis*. What does it consist of?

Through transference, that intense affective relationship Freud speaks about, we reproduce the type or types of relationship that we have with others. These are types of relationship that are not directly or easily readable in our behavior because they are governed by very old and forgotten experiences, active or passive, which have been transformed into phantasms rich with meaning. By contrast, in the artifact of transference, rather like in a laboratory, we repeat our mode of functioning in regard to others in the pure state. We do so in the pure state because we are freed, on the one hand, from the reactions of others that oblige us to hide or disguise our thoughts and actions, and, on the other hand, from responsibility for our acts and our words, at least for a time. But the description I have just sketched provides only one side of transference. If this were the only side to play a role, the revelation of our mode of functioning would be illuminating and, if we couldn't stand this revelation, we might go mad (as sometimes happens), or, if we could stand it, it might profoundly change our mode of relationship.

Yet there is another side to transference that turns it into a neurosis: we are subtly attached to our mode of relational functioning, and we don't want to change anything about it, beyond its most apparent characteristics. I think it is necessary to explore this point further—and, to grasp its implications, to go back to an elementary experience we generally have during the first sessions with a patient. This patient explains to us that he is suffering from a certain number of symptoms and asks us to rid him of them, in a word, to cure him of them, but we soon realize that he simultaneously asking us not to get rid of them. If, in fact, the symptoms are present, there are good reasons for it—poor reasons, no doubt, but good nonetheless, for symptoms are useful and even necessary. They have been cleverly crafted to preserve something to which the patient is attached, stuck, hung up, and which he does not want to let go. It is as if a core of suffering and dereliction had been revealed through analysis and the patient was holding on to it as if it were his most precious possession, as if by turning his back on it he had to renounce his identity—in short as if his suffering, his unique way of suffering, was identical to his singular form of existence. As a woman patient once told me, "my suffering is my only wealth."

This cultivated suffering, which is the root of neurosis and which is, one might say, the symptom, would be totally unintelligible if we did not connect it to a mode of relationship to others. Preserving this suffering is the only way at our disposal of not separating ourselves from those who have recognized us even as they misunderstand us, from those whom we have asked to support our image when they wanted only a double, from those, finally, whom we have allowed to enter into ourselves and who have been destroying us. This suffering, which constitutes our very life, carries within it the ambiguity of any relationship, that of a love which is hate, that of a rejection through absorption, that of a penetration by dint of exclusion. There is neurosis because we are incapable of doing without this other who is persecuting us, because he is also the person who upholds us in existence. To phrase it in yet another manner, everyone oscillates between the desire for independence, for mastery, for responsibility, and the infantile need to return to a state of dependence, of irresponsibility, and thus of innocence.

It is this suffering in and through the relationship with another human that will be repeated in transference; it will thus appear clearly and, because of that, can eventually be modified. But because it constitutes the analysand in his very being, it cannot be abandoned. Quite the contrary: if transference proposes that this suffering repeat itself, if the psychoanalysis makes it believe that it is in its interest to repeat itself, it will comply quite happily, and the analysis will be nothing more than an occasion for plunging a bit further into neurosis, with greater lucidity, perhaps, but without hope of escaping. Nothing else but analysis is capable in our culture of intermingling the illusion of a desire that may finally become great with the bittersweet qualities of adult infantilism. When analyses last a long while, it is not rare for this suffering to end up destroying the analysand's existence.

Some of you have certainly had occasion to see patients who, after ten or fifteen years of analysis, were in the deplorable state of those who have lost everything: their money, their job, their spouse. The power of the analyst to whom they entrusted themselves has literally destroyed their minds, and they admit that they are caught in a trap. After a few years of analysis, during the period when they had been able to notice a certain improvement in their state, when they had thought about putting an end to their analysis, the analyst had given them no reply to their desire to leave beyond an eternal "You must continue." Because they were waiting for the agreement of their analyst in order to leave, and because the analyst did not seem to be able to say anything more than that on the subject, they were forced to enter into an ever more extreme dependence. Their suffering was thus encouraged to spread, along with their inability to see the value of their own feeling that it was useless to pursue the analysis and their inability to draw the obvious conclusion from the sense of being powerless to assert themselves as individuals responsible for their own destiny.

I am well aware that, in certain cases, this refusal by the analyst to decide about the end of analysis, or to encourage it, can be a beneficial provocation, but that supposes, precisely, that the people involved are still to some degree capable of living their lives by themselves and of judging what is good or bad for them. Now we know that indefinitely prolonged analysis may harm such a capacity. Placing one's future in the hands of someone else is tempting to many people. The question did not arise in Freud's era because analyses then were often quite brief; but, in my opinion, it confronts us today in an urgent manner.

I will take up my third question by asserting that analysis must have an end. I am thus opposed to the adage that is constantly repeated in analytic circles, or at least in the one I know: "The longer an analysis lasts, the more beneficial it will be." We can see from the facts that this is not at all true, but for the French facts don't have very much importance; what matters is that the theory can retain its prestige. How, therefore, can one attempt to conceive of this contrary assertion: "Analysis must have an end"? Analysis is, I contend, like a fruit that one has to know how to pick at the right moment: if you pick it too early, the fruit will not have had the time to ripen; but if you do it too late, it will rot.

Let us go back to the question raised about the resolution of transference. Some people claim, as I've often heard, that there is no analysis possible without transference. But we have to ask ourselves what we mean by transference. Does it involve the relationship with a particular analyst with whom one has done one's analysis? This transference may, in fact, turn out to be difficult to break, but this transference to a given analyst does not appear impossible to dissolve if one considers transference as an intense relationship to a function—that is, to a multiform figure who allows dreams, phantasms and drives to appear in speech. At the end of an analysis, the patient no longer needs to have this function embodied in a woman or a man. After a time, when the analysand perceives that he is alienated by an other, by any other whatsoever, he becomes capable of appropriating this alterity for himself and he can learn to live in this alternation of alienation and appropriation. He has integrated the function within himself.

In other words, if transference is considered to be the constitutive relationship to one's other or to others—for we are innumerable—and if transference is considered to be a constant awareness of one's own genius, in the traditional sense, or of the geniuses that mark one's particularity or (to be more precise) one's singularity, there doesn't appear to be any need to detach oneself from it. In this case, there is no end to transference, but there can be an end to analysis in the sense of an effort to work through dreams, phantasms, and drives—that is, the end of a study or an attempt to explain one's behavior and thoughts, whether it be an effort at interpretation or comprehension. Remaining in the circle of the dream or of the analytic situation (for it seems to me that they are, in the end, the same thing) means transforming the reality of existence into an exercise or performance of narcissism.

I would like to elaborate briefly on this question. The need for an analyst is the need for an other who accepts the analysand, who recognizes him, who understands him, who tolerates him, who never judges him. Ultimately, it is the need for someone who supports his narcissism and who thereby communicates to the analysand the strength to live, who upholds him in his existence. Soon, however, this need is transformed into tyranny: if the analysand cannot do without that particular analyst, the latter becomes the person who holds within himself the secret and the condition for the former's existence. The analysand is alienated in the analyst as he was in the drives, phantasms, or desires of which he was unaware. And if he undertakes an analysis to make those phantasms disappear, then, at that moment, he is obliged to rely on the relationship with that other in order to subsist, which is merely a renewal of narcissism. If the analysand always needs the analyst to sense or recognize his drives, phantasms and desires, then the latter becomes the sine qua non for them. The analysand exists only through the analyst; he lives in the need to be heard, seen.

Narcissism could be defined as the need to hear one's self oneself, to see oneself as Narcissus, to understand oneself or love oneself, and it is undoubtedly in this way that certain analytic cures progress and conclude. Some people say that it is a question of curing the analysand of a lack of primary narcissism, and this is certainly something that is extremely important. Therapy may therefore consist of producing or making possible this primary relation to oneself that has been lacking, through the gaze or the ear of an other: the analysand may have been lacking that unqualified admiration that makes a person's existence unique, singular. This is what must be restored and what, in certain cases, psychoanalysis succeeds in restoring or even in establishing, which is altogether positive and altogether important.

I would, however, like to go a bit further, because narcissism remains a disease, a disease in the relationship to one's self as an other, in the relationship to one's self as well as to one's own dreams, and we can see in analytic circles or at the end of an analysis people who are, in fact, very narcissistic. This is, perhaps, precisely the height of analysis. It is Caesar preferring to be first in his village rather than second in Rome; it is Freud as Hannibal besieging Rome, or Darwin humiliating the human race. The narcissistic dream is always a dream of totality and a dream of infantile omnipotence. The height of narcissism is the height of relationship. The height of relationship is universal domination.

There is, perhaps, an end to this end of analysis, an end to domination, an end to the height of relationship, an end to the need for any relationship to others and to oneself. The greatest cure in the greatest disease is the hope-despair of solitude. This would entail not only no longer needing to be seen, heard, and loved—which would be the minimal state for smothering the neurosis, the zero point that kills all vague impulses toward neurosis; it would also entail, on top of or underneath that, no longer needing to see oneself, to hear oneself, and to love oneself, which seems absurd. It would mean breaking off all relationships, not only with others but with any other and with oneself, the end of Narcissus, the end of oneself, the end of duality, the end of division—the famous division of the self: the division of the West that wants to be seen or that looks at itself for lack of being seen, that wants to be heard or that listens to itself and understands itself for lack of being heard and understood; and, on the other hand, of the East that looks, to be lost in the gaze that I (probably only a minimal "I") cast upon others and on the world. At this point, the end of analysis, the cure is the beginning of the East.

This is obviously, in return, the condition for any and all relationships. The person who does not look at himself and worry about being looked at is a gaze and makes all things exist through the attention he pays to them, but he would not be able to reflect. There is no reflection in this gaze that gives itself over and loses itself in what it perceives, this gaze that does not come back to itself, this gaze whose contemplation is lost in the thing contemplated without any possibility for taking itself back, for recovering itself, or even for appreciating itself. It is, perhaps, the gaze of poets and gods: in Delphi at sunrise, or in the Abruzzi in April, the perfect light that gently embraces the contours of objects, or, as Goethe put it, "the eternal process of highlighting, the eternal process of giving life value and making it live."

There is no question that interpretation is necessary, that we must understand and think and reflect and read and comment; otherwise we would, of course, become first-degree imbeciles, uneducated people incapable of grasping the nuances of colors or of ideas. We must, therefore, accumulate readings and writings, and never stop describing, explaining, and reasoning. But, in analysis, there comes a time when the new life that is circulating tends to invalidate the most scholarly dissertations; there comes a day when interpretations seem ridiculous in comparison to what is in the process of happening. What counts at that moment is not interpretation, but change. What kind of change does this involve?

I would like to suggest this rule: the end of analysis begins with change in the analyst. A woman analysand told me some time ago: "If only I had any hope of changing you a bit!" (this person is perhaps borderline, somewhere between a neurotic and psychotic). This wish may be the wish of a hysteric who wants to leave her mark or trace in order to know that she is unique. But in this case it is the wish that the other, the interlocutor, will accept something from her without making any claims, without shutting himself off right away, perhaps the acceptance of a gift; and we know that our analysands give us a great deal. The supreme gift is the one that operates in the relationship through an internal change in this relationship and thus in the protagonists. It is a demand for a change that can also be tied to the fact that the analysand wants to be heard. "If you, psychoanalyst, hear me, you will be changed."

More radically, what matters is accepting a possibility for change. When a person who is not initially in the process of seduction utters the words "if only I could change you" perhaps as a cry of despair, or a cry of hope, she is essentially saying: "If I brought about a change in you, that means that I could bring about a change in this other being who is within me and who, within me, alienates me. I would have already brought about a change and the transference neurosis would have been attained." Or she might say: "This stereotypical form of relationship to others that I have been carrying around with me since I was born has already been changed if I have been able to change you. If I hold over you the power to change, then my relationship to my other has also undergone a change." Hearing does not mean understanding or interpreting; it means entering into the genesis of change.

Hearing also means being affected and undergoing the effect of a work of art, a life, a person. It is undoubtedly difficult to conceive of this experience: Might it involve a closure of the unconscious in the sense of a pronounced repression, a more total closure that could not have existed before the analysis? That is possible, for it is always easy to be wrong about oneself. But might there not be another form of closure of the unconscious? A non-reflection, a non-gaze on oneself, an unconscious that finds it henceforth useless to speak, that no longer feels the need to transmit something about its state, that is content to live what it has to live? Or, to use Winnicott's expression, an unconscious that is taking time to integrate affects? Thanks to analysis, this unconscious has found its own laws, which are not the laws of the separating and reductive intelligence. It is an unconscious that no longer wants to be alienated through interpretation, first of all because every interpretation is partial (in both senses of the word) and thus indefinite. More radically—and here we return to the conflict between knowing and curing with which we started—the unconscious no longer wants to be alienated through knowledge. In fact, the analyst's or the analysand's effort to know always operates in regard to the thing that he has initially frozen, the thing he has made rigid, the thing he has killed. There is, I believe, a closure of the unconscious that resembles respect for life, the kind of closure that acts in silence. One could consider psychoanalyses that go on forever as processes that transform the patient into an open victim: like birds that are ritually sacrificed, they should allow the oracle to interpret signs over and over again, whereas there is no longer anything to understand. As an American friend put it, "What pleases me is allowing life to take its course." That could be a maxim for psychoanalysts.

Chapter 13
A Condition of Liberty

Neutrality could be defined as a position of balance between forces going in opposite directions that, for this reason, are in an optimal state of availability.

Let us try to open up that definition. Opposing forces can be understood as forces that are directed either forward toward the future, or backward toward the past, and thus as forces of progression and regression. In an analytic cure we are dealing with forces of this sort. The dependence in which the analysand places himself tends to make him return to the infantile state, but this regression would have no meaning unless it were aimed at projecting him toward the future, toward a future, toward an existence that could be a bit more the result of a history and a bit less the effect of a destiny. It is not possible for these forces to be available with a future in mind if they were not first rediscovered in the form they assume in the infantile state, that is, if the subject in analysis has not come to seek them out and take them up again in the place where they have remained in their repetitive fixity. Some forces have been chained in the past; one must return to them in order to liberate them. They were dead, and one must bring them back to life so that they can be used with the future in mind. Like Orpheus, one must descend into hell and find the path that leads out of it.

When we use the terms regression and progression, we are applying them, first of all, in the temporal sense, and quite often we don't go any further than that. In reality, these terms should, according to Freud, also be given two other meanings: topical and dynamic. What appears to us to belong exclusively to the diachronic register must also be understood in the synchronic register. A temporal regression can ultimately be unnecessary, if the topical regression is carried out, for the most important thing is to discover or dredge out the place where suppressed forces are lying in wait. The past is that which, at the present moment, is imprisoned in death. The regression goes from being topical to dynamic if what one encounters in that place are really forces that are usually unknown. The return to the infantile state cannot be the point of departure for a change, if it is not actualized as upholding the present structure of the individual. Comments made in analysis that regard solely the present can have as much therapeutic effectiveness as the evocation of childhood memories, at least if the mention of the present goes so far as to bring forth, in the here and now, the forces of infantile nature—that is, the forces that make themselves manifest through dependence, through memories, through affects, through drives, and through the imaginary, the instinctive, the perceptible, the animal.

We know that regression, even if it were accomplished according to these three figures (the temporal, the topical, and the dynamic), cannot in itself become the source of a change. Hence the necessity of passing through a neutral point, through neutrality. The neutral point is the passageway between the past and the future. Why must there be an individual existence, why must there be a moment that is perceptible as such? One answer is because this is the moment when regressive forces are no longer experienced or imposed as an imperious necessity but rather are gathered, placed into a state of expectation, transformed into potential energy. It is only through the formation of this state of neutrality that the analysand is capable of seeing these forces truly placed at his disposal. If a force is liberated from the isolation that the symptom imposed on it, it is because it has already been integrated into the other parts of the individual and is becoming available energy. Now, this energy cannot be available if one has not supposed a time and place where it is received as such before being directed toward an action. The neutral point is the point at which forces are mobilized.

What is the interest of this point of neutrality in the cure, whose essential operation consists in drawing upon the past in order to move toward the future? This point designates the possibility for freedom. One goes from the past to the future through decision— that is, by abandoning the infantile, which is always the dream of keeping everything, and by choosing this and leaving that aside.

Decision is a madness, as Kierkegaard said, because it is a leap into the unknown and into novelty, more precisely because it is a loss that one is never sure can be compensated. Leaving the infantile state for humanity involves tolerance for a loss. It is this loss that is at the heart of any decision. Yet how could the loss be possible if the potential energy was not superabundant, if it did not make one sense that the loss is nothing compared to the wealth of what is opening toward tomorrow? People who do not choose are not engines running on low-grade gas, as Georges Bidault said of Robert Schumann. Rather, they are afraid of losing everything if they lose something. Decision thus supposes generosity, which supposes the conviction that the expense will not exhaust one's forces, the certainty that losing is the best way to win. Only this passage through the point of neutrality can give one this conviction and certainty. This point then becomes the condition of liberty; it is another name for what was traditionally called free will. If one does not pass through this state, as the place where potential forces are concentrated, there is no loss possible and thus no choice, no decision that traces in the present the path to the future.

You may, perhaps, think that I am straying from the subject by talking about the analysand's neutrality, when the theme at hand is that of the analyst's neutrality. It is, however, the latter that I was just addressing, in the sense that the condition of possibility for the analysand's neutrality is the neutrality of the analysis.

How can we describe this phenomenon? If he is alone, the analysand remains trapped in repetition. It is because he is tired of this that he comes and asks us to get him out of the vicious circle in which he is imprisoned. We may think that it is enough to interpret in order for the analysand to become conscious of his repetition and turn away from it. But things do not happen that way. We must, in fact, ask ourselves what this repetition consists of. What the analysand is repeating is quite simply the relational trauma that defines him: that is, the form of relationship with others and with the world to which he was constrained by his first family circle. Not having any other model available, he has internalized it and gotten into the habit of reproducing it. How can we break this spell? It cannot be done through words, however pertinent they may be. Since the form of relationship is so firmly rooted that it merges with the form of existence, only a different relationship—that is, a reality of the same structure—is capable of bringing about a modification. Even if we suppose that some words are effective, they will be so only if they are grafted onto the new relationship.

What then is the task of the psychoanalyst? It is to establish a relationship that makes possible the appearance of this point of neutrality in the analysand. That supposes, first of all, that the analyst himself experiences this neutrality in his relationship with the analysand. If he is not capable of staying in balance between the past and the future, between what is imposed and what can happen, between what is endured and what can be produced, if he can't concentrate his forces and maintain them in a state of expectation, then his presence will carry no weight in making the analysand feel the possibility of this balance, of this concentration and this expectation. Yet this neutrality of the analysis, when it is grasped from the perspective of the relationship, takes a particular form. It will be the stable passageway between two extremes: intense participation and identification with the analysand on the one hand, and distance-taking and objectification on the other. If the psychoanalyst is not caught in the net of the analysand, even if it is unconsciously and for a short while, then there will be no relationship and thus no change; but if the analyst does not stay in the background and does not lead the experience, even if it is after the fact and in a later stage, there will not be any change then either, because the relationship will retain its appearance of immediacy and thus of blind repetition. We can therefore see here that neutrality is not to be confused with staying out of things or with indifference; rather, it is the capacity to play with contrary forces.

The analysand is going to defend himself against this neutrality imposed upon him by the analysis. He wants, in fact, to be able to repeat his relational trauma. Moreover, as he is henceforth tied to the analyst, he does not want to break off the relationship. He can break it off, and that does happen at times, but it may also happen that the analysand doesn't want to. In this case, he is caught in a contradiction: if he resists, he is separated from the analyst; if he does not resist, he is forced to change his mode of relationship. It is thus out of this contradiction that his neutrality will be able to emerge. He can settle for oscillating between one extreme and another, that is, complaining that the analyst has abandoned him or conversely, seeming to change with the sole aim of pleasing the analyst. But this oscillation, at least in favorable cases, should not last if the analyst continues to hold his role and his place.

How can the analyst's neutrality, in the sense I sketched above, be a preparation for the analysand's neutrality? In the state of neutrality in which he is supposed to be situated, the analyst is reduced to a force in waiting, a force that is not tied to actions to be undertaken, to particular thoughts or feelings. This force is a pure possibility, which does not carry any determination with it. It presents itself to the analysand so as to meet the same force in him, that is, the same possibility. It imposes nothing that is determined or particular, which is not to say that it imposes nothing, since it opens for the analysand the space particular to his own possibilities. The analysand experiences this force, which forces him to draw out of himself a similar force, so that he may show his own resources. In that sense one can say that analysis is, in essence, a power struggle.

Yet we must be very clear about the meaning of that term. We are not talking about a combat in which each of the adversaries must impose his own thoughts and his own wishes on the other. Every time something of this sort is practiced between humans, we find that a power relation has been established. What I am trying to evoke could be called a relation of strength, of liberty to liberty, of possibility to possibility. Strength is force as a pure potential energy, and that is what is given in neutrality. Presenting oneself in strength means obliging the other to situate himself in his own brand of strength as well, at a level below that of any action, thought, or feeling. The analyst's power can thus be understood as the constraint imposed on the analysand to take his place and allow the possible to happen. It is thus admittedly a provocation, in the etymological sense of the term: that is, an appeal to be answered. In his neutrality, the analyst does not transmit anything he might have in his possession, for he does not have control over his liberty; he receives it and can only prepare himself to receive it. On the other hand, if he cannot transmit, he can at least incite the analyst to leave what he is, to experience the exact measure of his liberty.

What is at the heart of analysis is thus the capacity to come to a decision. This is not a perspective currently pursued by psychoanalysts. Freud used the word *decision* on several occasions. For example, in his *Introductory Lectures on Psychoanalysis* he used it to explain that if a decision has led to a disease, another decision must open the paths to the cure. If we accept this way of envisioning the individual's relation to his disease or to his cure, there will be no more question of attributing our misfortunes to our parents or to some person in our initial family circle; the issue now will be to recognize that we have decided our misfortunes. There will be no possible access to neutrality—that is, to the power to choose the future—if we do not begin by taking responsibility for our history. We can undoubtedly think that we have been the victims of various influences, but we cannot stop at this acknowledgment of blamelessness. It is we who have chosen to settle into this state of victim, and we could have made another choice. By retracing our history we can make new choices in it, situate ourselves differently in relation to it and, in the process, become the sole person responsible for it. The forces that we experienced passively are henceforth available to us, allowing us to transform our existence.

However, once again, this assumption of responsibility by the analysand, through which his neutrality is defined, will be made effective only in relation to the analyst's neutrality. The analyst carries his full weight in this relationship because he is free, because he himself, and to the degree that he himself, has his history at his disposal. If the analysand does not change, that is because he has found in his analyst certain dead forces that are the correlates to his own and that allow him to repeat his relational trauma. To paraphrase a formulation from Lacan, the analysand's resistance to change rests upon the homologous resistances in the analyst. Everyone knows that one chooses a given analyst to do an analysis, but also in order not to do one, because one has perceived with an infallible insight from the very first session that, with this analyst, certain brutal interrogations can be avoided. Any change in the analysand thus supposes a change in the analyst: that is, a step further toward neutrality, as it was defined earlier.

Before drawing certain conclusions out of what I have just said, I will develop some objections that could be made. First, am I correct in observing that there are forces present in analysis that go in opposite directions, some turning us toward the past, and others toward the future? I will leave aside the questions that one could call metapsychological (for example, what is this notion of force? Is it true that such forces exist? Is it correct that, by nature, they could be going in contrary directions, or might their supposed orientation be due instead to the way they are used?). I will limit myself to noting that analytical literature speaks most often of regression and repetition, that is, in reference to the past, and thus leaves in the shadows what could relate to the future; for regression and its passage into consciousness are judged to be capable of a renewal, or the future of the analysand is typically considered to be a matter that concerns him alone. But we will then have to explain why this recourse to the past is sufficient and, consequently, what are the goals pursued by psychoanalysis.

Next, is it legitimate to focus the experience of analysis on the possibility and the exercise of decision, as I have done? Psychoanalysts undoubtedly think that they are respecting the patient's freedom by intervening as little as possible and by letting him speak as he pleases, while taking care not to introduce in their interpretations words or expressions that this patient has not used himself, avoiding intervening in reality and not trying in the least to adapt him to the surrounding world. But can't we then raise two questions in this regard? First, doesn't the analyst's extreme reserve, which refuses to open up the future in any way, have the result of pulling the patient into a regression that goes in all directions, and whose dangers are by now well known? Regression, in and of itself, is incapable of bringing about changes; it leads to repetitions within and outside of the cure.

Finally, doesn't haughty respect for the patient's freedom lead to an attitude of *laissez-dire* and soon of laissez-faire, which is enervating and debilitating? If we think that the passage through the neutral point is not necessary—that is, if it is not the effective condition of liberty—then is what we are defending anything more than a formal liberty, a liberty devoid of any content, and which cannot, therefore, ever be exercised? Can a liberty be real outside of a relationship to another human, who is likewise capable of a similar liberty? As long as one refers only to formal liberty, one leaves the door open to all forms of power; and psychoanalysis is quite far from having gotten rid of them.

On that subject, we should not forget that we are no longer living in the cultural conditions in which psychoanalysis was born. One of Freud's aims was to loosen the stranglehold of a system of oppressive values by returning to drives. At the time, this effort seemed sufficiently liberating for patients to benefit from it spontaneously. In a world where collective imperatives—religious, philosophical, moral, political—have disappeared, and where the individual is left to the solitude of his own bearings, isn't it conceivable that we might raise the question of knowing what can be the outcome of a technique that is directed by free association and oriented toward understanding?

Moreover, when, outside of official meetings and far from the eyes of the high priests who watch over the purity of the ideology, we speak of the difficulties of our work and our efforts to find a solution, it clearly appears that we are straying from the so-called purity of analytic rules. But then we have a guilty conscience and we take great care not to make our practices known in public. Ferenczi was already talking about the hypocrisy of analysts; it has not stopped spreading since then. What we are lacking is the will to confront these questions directly and to try to think differently from the way we do. In recent articles or books written by analysts who have sought help from other techniques, one sees a concern with justifying their infidelities through oratorical caveats or through exaggerated theoretical developments derived from psychoanalysis. For these authors, psychoanalysis represents an impassable summit that has nothing to learn from anyone, such that these other practices, of which they are nonetheless asking something, are presented as never being able to be anything but a pale reflection.

If one accepts what I asserted earlier, it seems to me that we could follow another path. What I think should be situated at the heart of the analytic cure could well be claimed by other therapies. If that were the case, a certain dialogue could be established between them and psychoanalysis. We could then, without a guilty conscience and without hypocrisy, benefit from their contributions. That would obviously suppose that we stopped considering psychoanalysis as the Mecca of every possible therapy and that we review its limits—in short, that we abandon our self-importance. We are so thoroughly victims of the dominant ideology that we do not dare think what we are thinking secretly. As a result, we don't understand in the least the questions that come to us from other quarters, questions that are no doubt sometimes phrased awkwardly and naively, but that have all taken root and grown from psychoanalysis, thanks to psychoanalysis, and because of its limits.

You may know that several so-called new therapies have resulted from the work of Milton H. Erickson, such as indirect hypnosis, systemic analysis, family therapy, and so on. He was particularly the thinker who inspired Gregory Bateson. The fact that the French are unaware of these names may be understandable, even though they are no longer unfamiliar with the latter, nor with the School of Palo Alto, whose influence most particularly marked Harold Searles. What is stranger, and what in my mind seems to characterize the insularity of the international analytic circle, is that out of twenty psychoanalysts interviewed in different regions of the United States, not a single one knew that name.

Let us leave polemics aside. Given that it is impossible, in the present context, to develop the relations that could exist between psychoanalysis and other therapies, I would like to settle for opening the path to possible modifications in our technique on two particular points that I would qualify as follows: welcoming *the symptom* as a gift, and putting *the imagination* to work.

According to Freud, we must not treat the symptom directly, but rather return from the symptom to the resistance through interpretation. A more widespread technique consists in not worrying about the symptom and waiting for free speech to overcome it, in addition. But isn't it also possible to consider the symptom as an element that is suffering from isolation? Through its cumbersome and inhibiting insistence it reveals that an element of the psyche has been set apart and is not communicating with the other elements. It is thus a matter of reintegrating it into the totality of the psyche. This is possible to the degree that the patient stops treating it like a factor of persecution and receives it, accepts it, desires it as something that is indispensable to him and that carries a force he needs. Through what I will call a decision of reintegration, the symptom loses its exterior character; it changes in meaning and becomes a necessary part of the psyche's overall functioning. By no longer treating the symptom as an ill, by placing it once more under his own responsibility, the patient makes the force that had been used for the production of that symptom circulate once again.

Take, for example, a man who reproduces the nastiness of his mother, but doesn't want anything to do with it, who wants to leave it outside of himself. He knows, however, that this nastiness is the form of his bond to his mother. If, therefore, he changes his relation to this nastiness, if he perceives it as something that belongs to him and from which he does not want to be separated, if he recognizes and affirms it as his own possession, he ceases to be its victim, and it fades away in the process. There is nothing magical about this; rather, it is based on two presuppositions that are, I think, acceptable for an analyst: first, the symptom is an encystment in a part of the psyche; and second, the passage from a passive attitude to an active attitude transforms the relation to the symptom and reintegrates the force that supported it into the entire psychic life.

There is a second opening possible: putting the imagination to work. In analysis, we encounter the products of the imagination most particularly in the form of a dream, and we think that we must interpret this dream. We solicit the patient so that he will move from the images or words of the dream to an understanding of the dream's meaning. Wouldn't it be possible to consider the tale of a dream as something that carries an incipient desire? The analysand's task would then be to enter once more into the dream, like an actor who has played only one scene thus far and who is asked to continue the play. This sort of work allows the analysand not only to bring out more fully the desire or desires contained in the dream, but also to become the agent of a transformation in the dream's basic elements, in function of a future that he holds in his hands. What this entails is not finding the revelation of a hinter-world in the figures of the dream, as a Jungian analysis might accomplish, but rather changing the analysand's relation to his own imaginary world. There would be nothing magical about this either, but it would be based on the presupposition that we are continuously guided by the imagination, as a possible form of what we call the unconscious, and that this imagination can be worked or modified as such without appealing to an interpretation that would over-code it by giving it a meaning in relation to a general theory. Phantasms (a translation from the German word *Phantasie*, which is itself a transposition of the Greek word *phantasia*, always translated as *image* in Aristotle) can not only be experienced; the analysand can be the actor and the agent of their modifications.

Chapter 14

What Does It Mean to
Be a Psychoanalyst?

Psychoanalysis began on the day when Freud turned his back to suggestion and gave a voice to his patients in a context in which their speech proved to be effective. "Saying" had become a means of "doing," not in reaction to an injunction passed down from some authority or power, but through the force created in the very person who felt the need for a change. That meant that the effectiveness of speech was no longer the doing of the physician, but that of the patient, and that it originated no longer in the healer, but in the afflicted person.

On your own behalf, ladies and gentlemen [members of the Brazilian psychoanalytic associations], you have just performed the same founding act. When you selected as the subject of your gathering "Psychoanalysis, Identity and Difference," you became once again analysands of psychoanalysis, thereby performing the most beautiful gesture you can accomplish as psychoanalysts, even and especially if you have many years of experience. You have, in fact, spoken this theme and, at that very moment, put it in action. You have confirmed your differences from within an identity.

To get to this point you must have overcome many fears within and around you, fears of seeing haughty and discontented authorities awaken—authorities whose words are, precisely, hardly effective anymore—as well as fears of seeing your particularities disappear upon contact with other particularities. As if any meeting was a threat of dissolution, as if alterity was fatally destined to fade into sameness, whereas the authentic same is always the correlative to the other. The risk of differences crumbling originates in the weakness of our singularities, which are forced to hide themselves with a shiver unless they adopt rigid forms. The risk also arises from our claim to raise our singularities to the status of universal law, that is, to exclude other singularities and to take, with varying degrees of tact, a totalitarian route.

You have opened up exactly the opposite path by the choice you have made to set forth and carry out this theme of identity and difference in psychoanalysis. You have had the courage, so rare in our day and in our professional circles, of proposing the model that should govern every encounter of human individuals and every exchange among human groups: namely, the possibility of safeguarding and developing what is unique to each, in order to maintain and foster the sense of belonging to a single city, a single culture, a single humanity. In your capacity as psychoanalysts you have performed a political act, in the grandest sense of the term. For psychoanalysis and for this city that does not want to be led, but rather to lead (*Non ducor, duco*) [the motto of the city of São Paulo] this act will, I am sure, have the most felicitous consequences for the psychoanalysis of tomorrow.

In fact, it is not by chance, that your four institutions have chosen to hold this meeting under the aegis of the Instituto de Estudos avançados [Institute for Advanced Studies] of the University of São Paulo. *Estudos avançados* because it is indeed a question today of turning away from a past in which the fear of institutions forbid exchanges, and of going forward toward the future where cooperation will shortly override rivalry.

If psychoanalysis began when Freud established the conditions of effective speech for the analysand—that is, of a speech that acts—we must ask ourselves what those conditions were and what they still are in our eyes. If I raise this question in these terms, it is because I view it as a pertinent way of defining psychoanalysis, even if it is not standard practice to do so in this manner. In fact, it does not seem impossible to me that you may find it acceptable to think and say that speech is the favored means of the psychoanalytic cure. In psychoanalysis one does not move on to action, one talks. One talks and one listens. Nor does it seem impossible to me that you may find it acceptable to think and say that psychoanalysis must produce a transformation, thus that it must have its own efficiency. If one denies the analysand the right to substitute action for speech (what we call the passage into action), it is because his speech is already a move into action.

You thus agree on these few points. But it is likely that your agreement is surrounded, shadowed even, by countless questions. It is impossible to settle for a facile agreement that might hide several misunderstandings. If I want to talk about the effectiveness of speech in analysis, I will thus have to engage in a series of clarifications along the way, and it is here that the differences will appear in my way of explaining myself. Whose speech are we talking about? That of the analysand or that of the analyst? Can we place them under the same general and vague heading of speech? How is speech in analysis distinguished from the speech emitted in everyday life? How does this speech stand out? What is its relation to transference? Is this speech the expression of an affect? What is the nature of speech in interpretation, and where does it come from? What effectiveness can we expect from psychoanalysis? Does it involve a radical transformation, an improvement or a calming of symptoms? To this list of questions, I could add an even longer one.

Within this accepted identity—that is, the idea that psychoanalysis can be defined as the exercise of an effective speech by the analysand and, undoubtedly, by the analyst as well—I am going to try to express my personal way of understanding and developing this definition, which is perhaps different, perhaps similar. I would like to show that speech in analysis is effective first, because in transference, it is the verbalization of constitutive affects; second, because it is a decision; and third, because it invents the future.

Speech in analysis has a very particular nature. When, at the end of his *Interpretation of Dreams*, Freud describes the method necessary for analyzing dreams, he explains that one must allow unintentional and unwanted representations to emerge, and that it is a question of establishing a system of words that is arbitrary and aimless. Speech in analysis is thus nonsense speech, in the etymological sense of the term: it is not intentionally directed at a meaning, as human language must do and in fact does when it is spoken by people who want to communicate through words that have a meaning. According to the hypothesis formulated above, if speech in analysis is effective it is because of its particular nature, which turns out to be subject to nonintentionality. We would have to conclude from this that meaningful speech, the kind of speech that seeks to have meaning—in other words, intentional speech, the kind that we use all the time—is not effective, that it cannot be, and that it does not bring about what it means. Now, this is very much the case. Without entering into explanations that would take hours, if not days, we need only refer to our experience as psychoanalysts to recall that the coherent, rational, always controlled speech of an obsessional patient remains sterile, or that the trite complaints of a hysteric, who is waiting for pity in order to start complaining again, are expressed so that nothing will change. Effective words are those that translate these *Einfälle* (a word meaning "that which falls") from the German Romantic tradition, which Freud uses when discussing free association. It is this that occurs in the mind as if through a process of breaking and entering, it is this that comes to disrupt intentional speech, it is this that bursts in like an incident or like an accident and destroys the consciously intended meaning, it is this that turns our existences around and makes them take a different direction. Any effectiveness can thus be attributed to nonsense speech, and to it alone.

But in what ground or subterranean source do Einfälle originate? They originate in what we call affects or drives. Nonsense discourse, typical of speech in analysis and that we could just as easily call un-speech, is the expression of affects and drives. It is the expression of drives that show that we are a part of the world of the living, of affects that are the storehouse deep inside ourselves of all the relationships we have formed. Discourse must become meaningless because meaningful discourse was made to cover up what we are, to hide it from the sight of others and, first and foremost, from our own eyes. Speech can recover its force, thanks to transference, only if it renews contact with drives and affects, only if it is their exact translation. For its part, the analyst's speech will remain ineffectual as long as it is limited to proposing interpretations drawn from a code or a theory which the culture has long since assimilated and through which it presently protects itself. On the other hand, if the interpretation succeeds in formulating the present singularity of the analysand, or the particularity of the transferential relationship that is being experienced at that precise moment by the two protagonists, then the speech will express what is in the process of taking place. It is effective because it gives a human voice to what was, a moment ago, only a suffering buried in its own immediacy. But, in order for such a mode of speech to be emitted by the analysand, the analyst must not confine himself to a distant reserve but rather participate in the situation, such that the intensity of his investment produces the distance implied by his function.

Ferenczi remarked that psychoanalytic interpretation had the tendency of privileging the intellectual side of things. He noted that if free association is possible for the analysand only if he puts himself in a second state, close to the hypnotic state, then the analyst will, on his end, have to be in the same state to be able to speak what, up to that point, could not be spoken. Freud said that in receiving each analysand, we had to take care to forget everything we had learned; this was the only means of hearing the singularity of that analysand, a singularity that we had never encountered and that we would never encounter again. And he showed quite well in his case histories that he was capable of reinventing psychoanalysis on the basis of each of his analysands. Indeed, it is by abandoning the meaning we know in advance in order to enter into the confusion of drives and affects that a new meaning can be created. We experience in our practice, as the years go by, just how capable we are of acceding to the liberty that makes us hear each person in his way and in our way, a liberty that moves us away from the established dogmas, that makes us dare to take initiatives that are singular and indispensable to the pursuit of a cure.

Being a psychoanalyst, to respond for the first time to the question you have raised, means having your youth in front of you; it means letting the old people mull over their territories; it means marveling every day at the sudden appearance of unexpected words that transform an existence, and of strokes of inspiration that renew our understanding of beings and of the world.

Thus, speech in analysis is effective, first, because it is, on the part of the analysand as well as that of the analyst, the verbalization of constitutive drives and affects. Second, it is effective because it is a decision. How can an utterance, in itself, be a decision? In analysis, one decides to be what one did not yet know one was. When the utterance of an affect or drive that has dropped into our bodies or minds as if by accident (as does a slip of the tongue or a retort) reaches the point of upsetting the sense we had of ourselves, our initial reflex is to push it away as something that has arisen from someplace or someone else. Yet if we overcome our surprise and accept this utterance as our own, it is because we have chosen to see ourselves and situate ourselves differently than we did yesterday. Since drives and affects are only the external reading of our way of behaving and of being in the world, the decision to recognize them is therefore the acknowledgment of a position relative to the near or distant environment. Deciding means simply that we are appropriating a place that we did not know belonged to us, and that we were holding like an automaton incapable of reflection. Speech will be effective because it will transform destiny into history, because the surprising utterance that has become our attribute will change us in the very process.

A decision is often thought of as a decision to accomplish this or that whereas it is, first and foremost, a decision to adhere to what we are—that is, to take our particular place at the heart of the networks that constitute us. In Chaldea, two thousand years before Christ, soothsayers developed an encyclopedic discipline for analyzing omens in order to guide the choices of those consulting them. The key was not undertaking anything that would end up disturbing the order of the world. For that, one had to know the deciding party's exact position in relation to the current state of the environment. We have reduced the world to the narrow limits of the psyche, but our task remains the same. The psychoanalyst, as is indicated by the term Freud used so many times, must divine *(erraten)* the multiple determinants of the present and singular state of the analysand so that he will be able to place himself within that state in a renewed manner. It is not yet a question of orienting his existence in this or that direction, something that will come later, as happens to a ripe fruit; it is enough, for the moment, that he take active responsibility for what he had been enduring as an indecipherable necessity. In this sense—and I am answering, yet again, your second question—the psychoanalyst is a soothsayer, who brings forth in words the relational fabric in which the patient had been caught without his knowledge. He is the soothsayer who proposes to the person who is consulting him that he be today what he had already been without wanting to realize it. When we assert that an interpretation take its time in coming, being neither too early nor too late, we mean that in this particular instant the analysand is capable of deciding his speech—that is, of assuming the responsibility and burden of his own position in the complex whole in which he is placed today.

Psychoanalysis is thus the place for an effective speech, first, because it is the verbalization of affects and drives, second, because it is a decision to keep the place that the soothsayer has designated, and finally, because it invents the future. We sometimes hear that psychoanalysis is interested only in the analysand's past. Certainly, it is quite true that Freud underscored the degree to which childhood, and most particularly the experience of sexuality in the earliest periods of human life, were determining. It is also quite true that Freud made the recollection of the most distant days one of the principal tasks of the cure. Time and time again he maintained that neurosis was constituted before the latency period and that it was there that one had to look for the keys that could undo it.

However, it is impossible to think that psychoanalysis could remained confined to the investigation of the past. By the simple fact that it has given speech its original effectiveness it has opened up, in the present register of analysis, the paths of creation—that is, the paths to the future. We have forgotten that the technique of free association was a technique of invention imported from the field of literature. To recount how this idea came to him Freud referred, among other things, to a text by Börne, excerpted from a volume he had received as a gift for his fourteenth birthday. This text explains that to become an original writer all one needs to do is spend three days writing everything that comes into one's head, without stopping.

But the technique proposed by psychoanalysis is not specific to it; it applies to all forms of invention. Even in mathematics, as Henri Poincaré has explained so well, discovery is not the result of a deduction; rather, it is the sudden irruption, after long effort and when one was no longer expecting it, of a solution that merges elements that up to then had been foreign to each other. Through free association psychoanalysis therefore does nothing more than propose to every analysand that which is the privilege of creators in art or in science: namely, the possibility of giving new forms, not to bronze, sound, or matter, but to human existence. Every analysand is the artist or inventor of his own life, and for him, as for a painter or a scientist, every day can become a new dawn. The psychoanalyst can adopt as his own, in transposed form, the saying of Kubitscheck, the politician who founded São Paulo: *Tudo se transforma em alvorada nesta cidade que se abre para o amanhã.* ("Everything is transformed into dawn in this city that is rising for tomorrow").

There is no distance between invention and free speech. If unspeech is the expression of drives and affects, it will immediately be the force that upsets and reorients the direction of the river of our lives. For that, one must undoubtedly give oneself over to the anxiety of nonsense, of that which has never been seen or heard; one must approach the limit of the extinction of discourse in favor of images and silence, in expectation of the passage of the gods, whose return we can never certify. Inventing one's life, inventing so that the life of an interlocutor will be invented, means running the risk of losing oneself. The person who dares not do this will need certainties and conformities, muffled misunderstandings, unrecognized compromises. The person who confronts this may not end up with anything but endless doubt, constant self-questioning, and, as a bonus, a solitude that is both necessary and dangerous. We are well aware in our daily practice that no invention is possible except through the abandonment of the omniscience that is attributed to us and the recognition of our irremediable impotence. Like the painter who thought every morning that he had produced his last canvas the day before, or the writer who felt the same way about his last page, it seems obvious to us that, this time, inspiration will not come to us, that the task or the case is beyond our capacities, that no light is going to clear up the confusion.

From this we can grasp the idea that, although it cannot become a science, psychoanalysis is nonetheless close to one through the process of discovery. In no case can it transform its results, as mathematicians do, into apodictic formulas, nor can it propose experimental verifications as is the case in physics or biology. As René Thom remarked, the discourse of psychoanalysis will always stem from rhetoric, and thus from the art of persuading. For it can only generalize that which holds for a singular case and which, possibly and partially, can be applied to several other cases. It is incapable of providing irrefutable proofs for universal propositions. Thus, in this sense, psychoanalysis cannot by right or fact claim to be scientific.

On the other hand, if we consider science as it is creating itself—that is, at the moment of its genesis—then we find ourselves in the closest proximity to it. Indeed, the processes of invention are all similar. The fault of psychoanalysis, in the eyes of the sciences, is that it never leaves the stage of originating, the nascent state. But doesn't the distinction of psychoanalysis lie in the fact that it leads each of those who turn to it for help back to that moment when the waters recede to make way for the earth, to that time when out of the immemorial chaos a god brings forth the days, where the wandering of things and of beings ends through nomination?

To conclude, it is thus possible to propose a third definition for the psychoanalyst. The psychoanalyst is the person who is constantly becoming an analysand once more, the most modest and the most ambitious analysand. In our culture, isn't psychoanalysis an excellent means of becoming a seeker for efficient speech—in other words, perhaps quite simply a human being? From garrulous magic, which tries to make us believe in the power of its abracadabras, to the Christian religion, whose sacraments—the center of its practices—must bring about what they signify, and to science, which is correct only through the results of its procedures, the question of efficient speech has haunted humanity. It is as if, from the moment when humanity uttered the first word that marked its power, it had been filled with anxiety over the risk that the capacity which permitted it to name in order to live and survive would become detached from the thing it needed to apprehend. That is why it tries, all the time and everywhere, to put meaning where there may not be any. It is threatened with madness if words do not dominate its undertakings. It knows, however, that it must confront this danger so that it can draw the force of meaning out of the things that affect it. Efficient speech is the privilege of mankind, but will never be its property. Only the cunning, who know how to sense and respect the laws of this mode of speech, will be able to have access to it.

Chapter 15

Dream, Imagination, Reality

In the field formed by the disciplines that operate under the sign of the *psukhê,* two tendencies are in confrontation: on the one hand, psychotherapists want to expand the notion of transference to be able to use it as a means of conceiving the relationship they maintain with their clients; and on the other hand, orthodox psychoanalysts want to limit the use of the term *transference* to its appearance in the context of the analytic cure, strictly speaking. (The same thing is true, a fortiori, for the title of psychoanalyst.)

There are both practical and theoretical reasons for these divergences of opinion. The practical reasons can be characterized as commercial, for psychotherapists have an interest in claiming to act with the same instruments as psychoanalysts, with the latter supposedly occupying the upper echelon within the field of psychotherapy. Correlatively, analysts have an interest in guarding their territory and tracking down any poachers who remove any game from their lands through the use of their principal means of action.

The theoretical reasons arise from the principle of the dominant ideology. Psychoanalysis arranged things so that people would believe that it alone was capable of conceiving the psychotherapeutic relationship and that, through the concept of transference, it held the key to understanding that relationship. Psychotherapists have submitted to the same belief, and even though their work is distinguished from psychoanalysis in various ways, they do not see how they could do without the notion of transference as the basis of their practice.

To overcome this opposition, which threatens to be sterile because the same arguments are incessantly repeated by both sides, shouldn't we push psychoanalysts to define more clearly what they mean by transference, and urge psychotherapists to break free of their dependence or fascination with psychoanalysis by describing more relevantly what is specific to their practice?

If one wants to know what psychoanalysts think about transference, the best way to find out is to consult one of our best specialists in the area of Freudianism. I am referring to Jean Laplanche, who wrote a book on this very subject entitled *Le Baquet: Transcendance du transfert.*[1] The author notes there that analytic literature is trapped in a tautological circle: it defines the analytic situation according to the production of transference, and transference according to the phenomenon that appears in the analytic cure. To get out of this circle, which doesn't clarify anything, Laplanche proposes looking for models that might account for transference. The most obvious model is that of the psychic apparatus. This apparatus, whose elements are set forth in Freud's *Interpretation of Dreams,* is altogether the product of Freud's reflection on dreams. Through its obvious proximity to the dream, which appears during sleep, the psychic apparatus is first defined negatively by isolation, loneliness, disconnection in relation to the outside world. It is a self-enclosed system for which the question of reality or unreality does not even arise.

But why does Laplanche always place transference in relation to dreams? Quite simply because the analytic framework creates an artificial situation that, for the duration of the session, leaves external reality aside. This means that the analysand's relationship to the world and to others is no longer what it is in everyday life. The other whom the analyst constitutes, and who represents all others, does not offer the analysand any resistance, does not react to the comments he makes, and proposes no task for him to undertake. Likewise the imperatives of economic, social, political, moral, or religious life are lifted in the analytic situation. There is therefore no true alterity here, any more than during a dream, first and foremost because the specific language of this situation is not intentional language—that is, the kind that aims to communicate a meaning to an interlocutor. In analysis one doesn't really speak, for when one gives oneself over to free association one "un-speaks," since one says anything, leaving intention and will in abeyance, as Freud said; one therefore tends to approach a certain form of delirium.

Laplanche does not furnish these explanations, but they are assumed by the proximity he underscores between transference and the dream. This is why he considers it necessary to respond to the objection raised in *La Construction de l'espace analytique* by Serge Viderman, who argued that the self-enclosed nature of the analytic situation might lead to a total detachment from reality and that it should thus be characterized as a phantasm or fiction opposed to concern with reality.[2] Laplanche wants to answer this objection: in his view, the analytic situation should not be called fictitious, which implies unreality, because transference is the manifestation of the unconscious and the unconscious, according to Freud, cannot be put to the test of reality. One consequently cannot place the analytic situation in the category of fiction or illusion because it cannot be subjected to the proof of reality.

However, Laplanche is well aware that this answer is inadequate, that it is nothing but a metapsychological sleight of hand. Indeed, Viderman's objection never ceases to haunt Laplanche's book. After first appearing on page 83, it reappears on page 236, as if he had not yet answered it. If we suppose that the Freudian unconscious is not subject to the proof of reality—that is, that its manifestations cannot be contradicted by external reality, by the events of the surrounding world, by judgments drawn from experience—we are indeed obliged to ask ourselves from what sort of reality it stems. In this line of reasoning, Laplanche advances with baby steps.

The reality of transference, which is the reality in which the analytic situation unfolds, is, Laplanche tells us, the reality of the unconscious. Once again, however, we can ask of what the reality of the unconscious consists. The question is not impertinent. It shakes this more than three-hundred-page book and makes it tremble from end to end, without any solution to it appearing; for in the end, this unconscious is nothing more than the product of our imagination. It is not I who says that, but Jean Laplanche. I cannot avoid citing page 76 in its entirety, for this passage will save us from getting bogged down in useless precautions and open up an area in which we can think freely about the subject that interests us here:

The dream is a sudden opening or awakening onto the unconscious. The dream is not the unconscious, even if it functions very closely to it. What Freud shows is that the dream's *functioning* is very close to the functioning of the unconscious, very close to what we can *imagine* of a so-called primary process, of a process that would not be weighed down, nor held in check, nor inhibited, where thoughts would not be limited to a goal, a term, a pragmatic aim; but, in contrast to what we can *imagine* of the unconscious, the dream functions on the basis of contents that are not specific, that are what we call "diurnal remains," pieces of everyday life that are perfectly accessible to consciousness. The dream is thus a part of the preconscious that is subjected to the unconscious process, to the laws of the primary process; whereas we *picture* the unconscious or the "that" (but here we have no other model) not as a process but as something that includes contents that are proper to it; contents about which we can scarcely do anything but *conjecture*, since they are by definition repressed and extremely difficult to reach. But there are other differences between the dream and the unconscious, beyond this heterogeneity in their contents. Insofar as we attempt to *imagine* it, the unconscious's functioning is closed to the intentional dimension—that is, shut off from an opening onto a referent, an opening onto something other than itself. (my emphasis)

It is the intellectual honesty he has always shown that made Jean Laplanche write this liberating page. But, as is often the case in his work he asserts first truths that are very troubling for the small world of analysts, without being able to draw conclusions from them. This is quite understandable. For if Laplanche had displayed the content of his assertion that the unconscious is a product of our imagination, that would lead him very far from Freudian doctrine, which is by definition unthinkable. In the end, why should he wear himself out looking to determine what is the nature of the unconscious's reality when the unconscious is quite simply something that we imagine, that we picture, that we conjecture? However, from the moment he asserts that the unconscious has a reality and even a hyperreality the internal logic of Laplanche's serious investigation will lead him to discoveries of considerable interest for us.

The answer to Viderman's question gradually diversifies over the course of *Le Baquet: Transcendance du transfert*. Laplanche tries out a whole series of solutions. He refers, for example, to the text in the "Entwurf einer Psychologie" (1895) where Freud spoke of the excess of reality that the subject must confront.[3] Then he proposes that the infantile is hyperreal. He also suggests that the hard core of the unconscious might be the final and truest expression of our unconscious desires. The unconscious storehouse of this infantile experience would then be fundamentally tied to sexuality. Moreover, the author attempts to connect transference with phantasms, speech, and sexuality, with these three elements constantly intersecting.

But where, finally, do they intersect? Laplanche speaks of this only in passing, as if out of timidity, whereas he is taking a decisive step into a field that analysis seems to want to ignore, yet that can nonetheless allow us to raise again, in new terms, the question of the nature of the psychotherapeutic relationship, and thus of the nature of any relationship between humans. I will settle for quoting the passages in Laplanche's book where he opens this field but does not draw conclusions from it.

First, regarding the dream, he writes:

Another point where the dream cannot be considered as altogether equivalent to the unconscious is in its openness to the other, the dimension of communicating or addressing another. I spoke earlier about the referential dimension; now it is a question of the allocutionary dimension, the virtuality of a discourse being addressed to someone. Well, here again, we were envisioning the unconscious as closed, as a sort of discourse that was not strictly addressed to anyone, a sense phenomenon that had no referent but no addressee, either. Now, how about the dream? To be sure, it does not speak directly to someone; it has its autonomy, its own substance. . . . But, nevertheless, one cannot help noting that, from time immemorial, well before analysis and outside of it, the human being has had a veritable compulsion—mixed with an unquestionable pleasure—for recounting his dreams to others, for opening the dream up to another person. It is this spontaneous movement of conversion toward an addressee that, in analysis, becomes even more manifest, since the whole evolution of dreams over the course of analysis lies in the fact that they increasingly become an element of dialogue and, more generally, of relationship. (78)

Later, on the subject of games in Melanie Klein's analyses of children, Laplanche remarks: "The problem lies not with the substance of the discourse—its verbal, or perhaps, gestural material— but in the fact that it is addressed to someone: communication, allocution, and not simply behavior, even behavior endowed with 'meaning.' In other words, a game can be viewed as a behavior, but in certain cases, it can be an address, and this aspect is obviously the only one that interests Melanie Klein" (106).

Laplanche finally comes clean regarding that sexual infantile element that might be the hard core of the unconscious: "This *hyperrealism* may, deep down, be connected to that basic, impassable condition of infantile experience, which is constituted by the *hypersignificance* of this experience, that is to say the fact that the child's structuring capacities are overwhelmed by a profusion of messages to which he does not have the key, but which he knows are messages" (222, Laplanche's emphasis). To cite another example: "What I am trying, this year, to define is the way that the cure, or, in a more general manner, situations of transference resonate with this immersion of the young human being in a universe of significations that exist prior to him and go over his head, overwhelm him and traumatize him" (235). These messages or these significations received by the child may be emitted by the parents; they may in particular be the product of the mother's enigmatic sexual desire. Moreover, and on this point Laplanche is explicit, these messages may not necessarily be verbal: "They can be intraverbal or para-verbal" (234). They can express even though they are constituted by actions; they can even be, as we just saw with games, simple behaviors.

So you heard it right: the hyperreality of the unconscious, which is related to sexuality, boils down to messages that are received by the child and that he cannot assimilate. We are, therefore, not in the realm of the fictitious anymore, because the messages that have been received by the child are indeed real messages, verbal or nonverbal, that can be detected through what might be called either macro- or microperception. As a consequence, a certain reality can be given to transference. One may think that the analysand will transfer onto the analyst these messages that he internalized during his childhood.

The odd thing is that after all of these detours and all of these attempts to find a solution, Laplanche, hardly satisfied, ends up observing: "As you see, the reason I wanted to give such emphasis to the theme of the fictitious, and to the idea that analysis could be reduced to something fictitious, was that this question is still cropping up" (249). We are at the end of the book, and one might think that this theme had been adequately discussed. But that is not the case. Why, then, is this question still cropping up? It is undoubtedly because the culmination point of Laplanche's reflections cannot be taken into consideration in the psychoanalytic situation. Or, to put it differently, the psychoanalytic situation is designed in such a manner that this culmination point loses its meaning there. If we accept as the key to this entire debate the translation of the reality of the unconscious in terms of a message, then we will have to rethink the analytic situation differently and ask ourselves some questions as elementary as these: who, during childhood and now in analysis, emits messages and to what end; and who, in both cases, receives them? What, in fact, is a message that may not be addressed to anyone, or to someone who is anyone at all or nobody?

Let us return to the stakes of the debate. Laplanche would like to answer the accusation made by Viderman, according to which psychoanalysis may take place in a fictitious register. But perhaps this polemic has no reason for being. For it is easy to show that they are both right. It is quite true that psychoanalysis creates an artificial space and occurs without taking reality into account—on another scene, as Octave Mannoni put it, borrowing an expression from Freud. We move there after having set aside all of the imperatives of external reality, and it is indeed a question of fiction. Viderman is thus quite right. But this fiction is a reality; it is, for example, the sum of the memories of childhood seductions, as Laplanche describes it. Thus, in this regard, he is right.

The error they both commit is that they do not reflect enough on the simultaneously fictitious and real nature of this space. They also err in not considering the relationship between this fictional real and external reality, the reality of our lives in society. Yet as psychoanalysts confined to their discipline, perhaps they could not.

Let us try to take up the question in different and quite simply traditional terms. By what is our daily life dominated and informed? The ancestral answer, still valid today, is categorical: it is dominated by the imagination. Now, the power and the productions of the imagination are quite real, but not in the way that we understand it for external reality.

We can, for example, find the following passage in one of Aristotle's *Parva naturalia*: "Indeed, just as, when we are on the point of accomplishing an act, and when we are accomplishing it and after we have accomplished it, we think of it frequently and perform it in a veracious dream [*euthuoneira*] (the cause for this is that the movement is prepared by the elements gathered during the day), so, too, inversely, the movements that take place in sleep must often be the principles of actions accomplished during the day: the reason is that the idea of these actions has already been prepared in the representations [*fantasmata*] of the night." Thus the products of our imagination during the day are, like dreams, the antechamber of our action.

Centuries after Aristotle, Montaigne asserts in his *Essais*: "There is no cause needed to agitate our soul: a daydream without body or subject dominates and agitates it."[4]

Even closer to us, Casanova underscores at the outset of his *Memoirs* (as if he is stating a universal fact) that "Many things become real that previously existed only in the imagination."[5]

Finally, it was barely yesterday that we heard these comments by Emile Coué, who profoundly influenced your master, Charles Baudoin: "Every time there is a conflict between the imagination and the will, it is always the imagination that carries the day, and in this case, not only do we not do what we want, we do exactly the opposite of what we want, and the more voluntary efforts we make, the more we do the opposite of what we want."

One could even go so far as to show that it is not initially sensations that prepare perceptions, but hallucinations (but I don't have time to do that). For example, the infant who cannot yet distinctly perceive the world around him nonetheless knows it in its totality and in its differences, and he hallucinates it in that fashion in order to be able to grasp it distinctly. It is there that the imagination takes root, in a capacity to feel, to know, and then to act on external reality, which is given from the very origin and which will always be there before any action. This capacity is the reservoir of possibilities, it is a power, a strength, and a force that orients us and motivates us in all of our undertakings in society.

There is thus no need to defend ourselves against the fictitious or fictional quality that marks the analytic experience from start to finish. Indeed, that is what constitutes its value and effectiveness. It may simply be futile to cling to the term *unconscious*, used as a noun, since the term *imagination* does the job just as well and also carries a positive trait, saying something about its content, whereas the word *unconscious* will never be anything but the negative of consciousness and carries with it philosophical and practical difficulties that are nearly inextricable.

If psychoanalysts dread accusations that their enterprise is fictional, that is because they never really think about the relations between fiction and reality. I would make two sorts of related and opposed demands of psychoanalysis today: that it go further in asserting and realizing its fictional component, and that it articulate this fictional component and associate it in the cure with the transformation of existence. Indeed, we know, for example, that a psychoanalyst who is strictly faithful to Freud *on the one hand* does not wonder about the means of obtaining a state that could make free association possible and settles for asking the patient to say everything that comes into his head, and *on the other hand* that he is not interested in the reality of the patient's life, for he wants to remain on the other scene, that of the unconscious or, according to Laplanche, that of the dream.

For most of you, such a language will undoubtedly appear to be a caricature of your way of working. You'll tell me that psychoanalysts have long shown their reservations regarding the rules imposed by strict orthodoxy. I am willing to believe that, but it doesn't prevent us from conceiving as exactly as possible the situations that are provoked by different techniques.

I will thus return to the two demands I make of psychoanalysis. First of all, by what means should we prepare analysands for free association? That is, how can we create a state in which intention or will, according to Freud's own terms, no longer play a part, such that speech becomes un-speech? We are well aware that this is not easy. If many psychoanalyses turn in circles, that is because they do not leave the register of conscious thought, and because the command to say everything—that is, the command to freedom, whose paradoxical nature has often been noted—does not suffice to liberate the analysand's speech. To obtain this state, wouldn't it be possible to use the techniques of induction that are employed in hypnosis? This would not be illegitimate, given that Freud observed several times that the mainspring of hypnosis and that of transference were identical. Free association is the result of a state of relaxation and lack of constraint, and we should thus take the time necessary to create this state. When the psychoanalyst who wants to spur on the analysand repeatedly asks the question, "What are you thinking about?" he risks giving too much importance to the register of thought and control, whereas the question that arises when one has succeeded in putting someone in a state where intention and will no longer play their role becomes, "What are you feeling?" This inevitably orients work on the side of the emotions and the imagination.

The second demand concerns the relation to the existence of the patient. It has been said that the cure in psychoanalysis was something that came as an extra and that the analyst didn't have to worry about it. Undoubtedly, this allows the psychoanalytic adventure to be developed, but there are patients who are no longer able to return to their existence and whose life is absorbed by the psychoanalysis. We must find a means of combining these two aspects. That is what one seeks to obtain in hypnotherapy. On the one hand, one tries to create the artifice of relaxation and lack of constraint, and on the other hand, one tries to permit the patient to modify his existence little by little. Although hypnosis was, in the past, generally considered a state of pure receptivity that sensitized the patient to the commands of the hypnotizer, it is now seen as the departure point for transforming the patient's existence. Emile Coué, who working with Liébault in Nancy drew the best out of hypnosis, constantly repeated that there was no suggestion that wasn't a self-suggestion. Thus, as Milton H. Erickson repeatedly emphasized, there is no hypnosis that is not a self-hypnosis. What one teaches the patient to do is to cure himself, to change himself today to the degree he believes possible. The therapist is then a catalyst who makes self-healing possible.

It may seem to you that my speculations have led me far away from the question posed by transference, that intense relationship that goes from the analysand to the analyst. Yet it seems to me that we have ended up right there, and that we can now undertake a more extensive reflection on transference.

Let us return to Laplanche's hypothesis. Transference, according to his model, would be similar to the dream. But why does he make this analogy? He does so because, as we have seen, the analytic relation of couch to chair is cut off from external reality, because speech is no longer intentional here, and because we are on the other scene, the one that is said to be the scene of the unconscious. We speak there as in a dream, we no longer place a limit on the expression of our desires, our sentiments, or our thoughts, neither out of interest or usefulness, nor concern with an action, nor respect for the interlocutor. The only limit set is that of the interdiction on acting, and this only accentuates the resemblance between the analytic situation and the dream, for the dreamer, too, is forbidden to move.

But, you'll ask me, how does this relate to transference, since transference is a relationship to an other and you describe the individual in analysis as being without relation? The answer is clear: transference is a fictitious, fictional, unrealized relationship. The analyst is a person who is Nobody, like Ulysses struggling with the Cyclops. The analysand does what he wants with him, he projects upon him as he wishes all the people known and unknown whom he needs in order to say what is making him suffer or feel pleasure. It is for this reason that the psychoanalyst is said to be neutral, a face without a face. It often happens that an analysand doesn't know if his analyst is blond or dark-haired, whether he has glasses or not, whether he is big or small. The analysand has dreamed his psychoanalyst.

You are, however, well aware that the description I am giving here is of only one side of transference. Why is an analysand capable of getting under his analyst's skin with such unmatched skill, and why, at the beginning or the end of a session, is he capable of grasping the differences in the analyst's gaze or the nuances in his gestures? Why, in certain cases, are happiness or depression in the analyst communicated to the analysand with lightning speed? Communication in the analytic situation is, or can be, very intense — too intense. Too intense because it, too, is limitless, and because the psychoanalyst ends up taking a disproportionate place in the life of the patient, with dimensions like those of a sustained dream. As Freud said, the neurosis has changed into transference neurosis, a second neurosis to which it is quite difficult to put a stop.

From these facts we must conclude that the neutrality of the psychoanalyst is not neutral at all, or that his neutrality—that is, his withdrawal to a point below that of ordinary exchanges—takes the relationship to the extreme of its intensity. Neutrality, because it is established in the domain of dreams and imagination, becomes the quintessence of relation. It is for this reason, I believe, that it can become the point of departure for a change of existence—if it is true that the dream, through its messages, and the imagination, through its projects, determine existence in society. It is as if the psychoanalyst, by working his way into the structure of the patient's dreams and imagination, could renew their elements or the relation those elements maintain among themselves. Ultimately, if it is to be efficient and have meaning, neutrality supposes a maximum investment on the part of the analyst. Transference, as an intense relationship of the analysand to the analyst and of the analyst to the analysand, would no longer be merely similar to the dream; it would be predicated on the analyst's entering into the patient's dreams and imagination, a formidable kind of breaking and entering, in order to modify them from the inside. The analysand would no longer settle for pouring out a stream of phantasms and repetitive complaints that, in the end, remain unheard; rather he would accept, through this relationship taken to the height of intensity, a new twist to his existence.

Yet this way of envisioning things is perhaps improbable, for another trap opens under the feet of transference. According to Freud—and this has become one of the most popularized fables in psychoanalysis—transference has an invincible tendency to become transference-love. And, in this case, the analysis stops and no change is conceivable. Before we ask whether transference's precipitous shift into love is fatal, we must determine of what that precipitous shift consists. Transference is that powerful bond by which the analysand transforms the analyst into the other of his or her dreams, and thus into an other by whom he or she may be loved (or persecuted, which ends up being the same thing). It is thus the analyst's neutrality, the fact that he is available to don all sorts of masks, which causes transference to turn into love. But there is another fundamental trait that we should emphasize here: transference changes into love only through the surreptitious passage from the fictitious to the real. The analysand, no longer tolerating the artifice of the cure, sets the transference in action; that is, he or she makes it penetrate into reality. This act signifies a passage into action. The limitlessness of the transference, which fictively makes the other the object of every phantasm, is replaced with the effective reality of infinite love, and thus amorous passion.

If we now ask why all neutrality does not lead to amorous passion, the answer is provided by the description of the passage between transference and love. This shift will not be fatal, on the express condition that the transference remain in the realm of the fictitious. But how is that possible? If the fictitious aspect of the analytic situation was only a pure illusion, purely imaginary, its preservation would be untenable, for then sessions repeated over the course of many months would soon culminate in nothing but delirium (a solution that we know is not merely a theoretical case). It is therefore necessary that this fictitious aspect, as we discussed it earlier, become reality, a hyperreality. But what reality or hyperreality are we talking about? To answer that question, we must describe more extensively neutrality, which we just saw was at the origin of transference.

While being neutral I am, as a psychoanalyst, indifferent to everything that the analysand may say or feel. I open up for him the unlimited possibility of saying and feeling everything that may spring up within him. But indifference in this context does not mean disinterest or lack of investment. It is even the exact opposite. Neutrality is not an attention that is floating, in the sense of being vague, diffuse, or hesitant: it is an exclusive concentration on the other; it is receptiveness par excellence, active availability, openness to all the possibilities that may come to light. In a word, it means being at the analysand's disposal, an energy under tension, and, already, the communication of a power that will find in existence the paths to its realization. As an artifice, therefore, it is far more real than external reality; it is the force of pure existence that is not yet determined, but that contains within itself all the possible determinations.

I am sure that these observations are not abstractions for you, but rather laden with meaning from your daily experience, from the best aspects of what you propose to those who seek you out in a state of pain or disarray. Our analysands or our patients are not interested in our love, our sympathy, our commiseration, or our pity. What they come looking for is the source of energy, of force, and of power from which they have strayed or which they have never known. We can give it to them to the extent that, not wanting anything particular from them, we concentrate on ourselves without thought, without emotion, without desire, and even more so, without worry or anxiety, in order to return to the origin of our existence or more simply the fact of our existence. We position ourselves, we place ourselves there before them or next to them like trees whose roots extend deep into the soil, planted in the barest life, both spirit and earth, in a state of correspondence with everything and with nothing, as if we were at the beginning of the world, at the first morning.

That's all a lot of romanticism, certain people will think, and some of them will even go so far as to say, smirking, "that's all a lot of mysticism." They'll be right, and I willingly accept as truths remarks that they consider to be insults. Do you think that we could pursue our work very long if we weren't capable of establishing some sort of kinship with poets or visionaries? Our offices are not, after all, factories where we sit churning out consumer products. What fascinates us is making existence reemerge in someone in whom it had become bogged down in the mud or in the swamps. But how could we do that if we did not put ourselves, along with those who have experienced or proclaimed it, at the heart of the extreme poverty that gives everything because it has nothing, that possesses nothing because it wants to be able to be astonished at every moment that there *is* something, something rather than nothing? *Thaumazein*, the astonishment that is the mother of all science, as Aristotle said, or that, in words of Péguy, allows us to "swim back with the stream of being."

Notes

Preface

1. I thank Jean-Luc Fidel for having had the patience to read a mass of articles and lectures and to choose those that revolved around a recurring and evolving theme. He was also the person who suggested using this title—the only trace that remains here of a lecture I gave in Seattle in March 1987—for the book as a whole.

2. Letter of November 12, 1922, published in Groddeck, *Der Mensch* (Limes Verlag, 1970). At the time, Ferenczi was attempting to distance himself from Freud, and Groddeck was not yet under Freud's sway. Groddeck was making fun here of all the psychoanalysts who viewed Freud as the center of the world.

3. By focusing his reflections on contact, Jacques Schott set Freud back on his feet again with the help of Szondi; see *Szondi avec Freud* ("Bibliothèque de Pathoanalyse," Brussels: Éditions universitaires, 1990). Why should contact be privileged? It makes itself privileged because it is the basis of vital function. Aristotle, who ends his ΠΕΡΙ ΨΤΧΗΣ with several chapters devoted to touch, associates touch with the operation of the nutritive function—that is, the vital spirit in its greatest simplicity. Touch is the thing of which no living being can be deprived without taking away its life. Contact supposes the existence of this soul, this psyche, and it invites it. Psychic reality is, first and foremost, the reality of the sensation of touch.

4. Michel Henry, *Généalogie de la psychanalyse: Le commencement perdu* (Paris: Presses Universitaires de France, 1985).

5. See François Roustang, *Qu'est-ce que l'hypnose?* (Paris: Minuit, 1994).

Chapter 1. Nobody

1. See the introduction to Michelet's *La Sorcière*, where he asserts that the sorceress is the origin of science.

Chapter 2. Uncertainty

1. "In Germany, shepherds have won bets by recognizing every sheep in a herd of one hundred heads that they had only had for two days"; cited by Pierre Thuillier in "Darwin était-il darwinien?" in *La Recherche*, no. 129 (1982), 11.

2. Jacques Lacan, *Écrits* (Paris: Seuil, 1966), 247.

3. Freud, "On Psychotherapy," *The Standard Edition of the Complete Works of Sigmund Freud*, translated by James Strachey in collaboration with Anna Freud, assisted by Alix Strachey and Alan Tyson (London: Hogarth Press: 1953–74), 7: 258; "A Phobia in a Five-Year-Old Boy," *S.E.*, 10: 104; "The Dynamics of Transference," *S.E.*, 12: 100. All further references to the *Standard Edition* will be made in the body of the text using the abbreviation *S.E.* followed by the volume and page number.

4. *Les Premiers Psychanalystes: Minutes de la Société psychanalytique de Vienne* I (1906–1908) (Paris: Gallimard, 1976), 123. There is nothing original about these remarks by Freud; they are commonplace among practitioners of animal magnetism and among hypnotists. Cf. L. Chertok, "Psychothérapie et sexualité: Considérations historiques et épistémologiques," in *Psychothérapies*, 4 (1981), 215–22.

5. "Observations on Transference-Love" (1915 [1914]), *S.E.*, 12: 159–71.

6. *S.E.*, 18: 115 ("Mass Psychology," 1921). A bit further on the same page, Freud remarks: "It is interesting to see that it is precisely those sexual impulses that are inhibited in their aims which achieve such lasting ties between people."

7. "Son-mother (or mother-son) incest seems to entail a discourse that is far more hidden and poses a certain number of problems that we will only sketch"; Patrice Bidou, "A propos de l'inceste et de la mort," in Michel Izard and Pierre Smith, eds., *La Fonction symbolique* (Paris: Gallimard, 1979), 111. This is particularly true because the mother does not belong to the father-children lineage, which is the only type of lineage that expresses endogamy.

8. Françoise Héritier proposes a second definition for incest: "It is no longer a question of the relationship that unites two blood relatives of different sexes in a prohibited sexual relation, but of *the relationship that unites two blood relatives of the same sex who share the same sexual partner*. It is these blood relatives of the same sex, related as brother/brother, sister/sister, father/son, or mother/daughter, who find themselves in an incestuous relationship by virtue of having a common partner, and who put up with the attendant dangers"; "Symbolique de l'inceste et de sa prohibition" in *La Fonction symbolique*, 219. Héritier later demonstrates that the incest prohibition is decreed "when the notion of what is identical vacillates on the borders of difference" (232).

9. In *Mémoires intimes* (Paris: Presses de la Cité, 1981), Georges Simenon provides a nice example of effective incest, even though it is not realized sexually.

10. Note that prudish analytical literature prefers to speak of the phantasm of having a child by one's father, which, it is worth remarking, was nonetheless far more serious for ancient civilizations because the incest became visible. As Patrice Bidou observes, "The shame does not stem from the desire to sleep with one's sister, or even from the fact of really sleeping with her, but rather from the fact that it is brought to light. Or rather, that it [incest] escapes from the narrow frame in which it is defined: 'Incest is fine, as long as it's kept in the family,' wrote Claude Lévi-Strauss in his epigraph to 'Secrets de famille' "; "À propos de l'inceste et de la mort," 121.

11. Not all psychoanalysts, obviously. Cf. several articles in the special issue of *Études freudiennes* entitled "L'amour de transfert" (May 1982), especially the essay by Julien Bigras, "Retour à la scène du crime." See also Monique Schneider, *La Parole et l'inceste* (Paris: Aubier-Montaigne, 1979).

12. See note 10.

13. Everything that stems from the category of the unique can be attributed to incest. Georges Devereux notes that among the Mohave Indians, the only type of marriage that requires the consent of the parents, the only type that necessitates a ritual, and the only type for which society claims to forbid divorce is a marriage that takes place between cousins, which "constitutes an incest, in the strictest sense of the word"; *Ethnopsychanalyse complémentariste* (Paris: Flammarion, 1972), 188. Devereux continues: "If, therefore, we admit that the only 'true' Mohave marriage—that is, the only kind that, being ritualized, resembles marriage in other societies—is an incestuous marriage, one that is absolutely forbidden, it seems necessary to conclude that the function of the ritual of marriage is to legitimize the illegitimate, to support the unsupportable, to substitute an apparent benevolence for a real hostility. Marriage is sacred—that is, dangerous—precisely because it allows what is forbidden; it consecrates sacrilege" (188). It is easy to deduce from this that the indissoluble monogamous marriage that preoccupies our civilization is—indeed, seeks to be—the ritualization of incest. Didn't Saint Paul, who was the true inventor of this form of marriage, give as its model the union of Christ and the Church? The Church is traditionally and consistently symbolized as Mary, the Virgin Mary. The model of ritualized indissoluble monogamous marriage is thus the union of Christ and his mother. There are few religions that have been as audacious as this. Christianity can, therefore, not be accused of having forgotten incest. That, no doubt, is the source of one of its strengths: presenting the uniqueness of the bond between son and mother as a rule to follow in establishing the bond between man and woman must have been one of the foundations of the uniqueness of the individual human in our culture. This religion has nonetheless gone a bit too far in that direction. That may also be one of its weaknesses.

14. Françoise Héritier, "Symbolique de l'inceste et de sa prohibition."

15. Nicole Loraux, *Les Enfants d'Athéna* (Paris: François Maspero, 1981).

16. Patrice Bidou, "À propos de l'inceste et de la mort," 111.

17. Georges Devereux, *Ethnopsychanalyse complémentariste*, 169–99.

18. On this question, especially its strategic and logistical aspects, see the work of Paul Virilio, in particular *Vitesse et politique* (Paris: Galilée, 1977) and *Esthétique de la disparition* (Paris: Balland, 1980).

19. Elias Canetti, *Masses et puissance* (Paris: Gallimard, 1981).

Chapter 4. On the Epistemology of Psychoanalysis

1. Habermas, *Erkenntnis und Interesse* (Frankfurt am Main, 1988), In English, *Knowledge and Human Interests*, trans. Jeremy J. Shapiro (Boston: Beacon Press, [1971]).

2. E. R. Dodds, *The Greeks and the Irrational* (Berkeley: University of California Press, 1959).

3. Jean Laplanche and J.-B. Pontalis, *Vocabulaire de la psychanalyse*, 4th ed. (Paris: Presses Universitaires de France, 1973), English ed., *The Language of Psycho-analysis*, intro. Daniel Lagache and trans. Donald Nicholson-Smith (London: Hogarth Press, 1973).

4. Ludwig Wittgenstein, *Lectures and Conversations on Aesthetics, Psychology and Religious Belief* (Berkeley and Los Angeles: University of California Press, 1966), 51.

5. In Lacan, *Écrits* (Paris: Seuil, 1966), 879–87.

6. Regnier Pirard, "Si l'inconscient est structuré comme un langage . . ." *Revue philosophique de Louvain*, 77 (November 1979), 564.

Chapter 6. The Components of Freud's Style

1. Jules Lachelier (1832–1918) was a French philosopher.

2. *Philosophie*, 3 (September 1984), 47–66.

3. See Michel Henry, *Généalogie de la psychanalyse: le commencement perdu* (Paris: Presses Universitaires de France, 1985); translated by Douglas Brick as *The Genealogy of Psychoanalysis* (Stanford, Calif.: Stanford University Press, 1993).

4. Henry, *The Genealogy of Psychoanalysis*, 9. [I have slightly modified Douglas Brick's translation—Trans.]

Chapter 7. On Transference Neurosis

1. I am using here my own version of the distinction made by Michel Henry in *The Genealogy of Psychoanalysis*.

2. Eugen Herrigel, *Zen in the Art of Archery*, with an introduction by D. T. Suzuki, trans. R. F. C. Hull (1953; rtp. New York: Vintage, 1989).

Chapter 8. Pedagogue or Mystagogue

1. In Greek, *paidagōgos* signifies "he who leads the child"–that is, a person who takes the child by the hand to take him to school.
2. Odo Marquard, *Schwierigkeiten mit der Geschischtsphilosophie* (Frankfurt am Main: Suhrkamp Verlag, 1973).

Chapter 9. Transmitting Anxiety

1. Maurice Dayan, "Le devenir-inconscient de l'autre chose," *Études freudiennes*, 29 (April 1987), 17.
2. Søren Kierkegaard, *The Concept of Anxiety*, trans. Reidar Thomte (Princeton: Princeton University Press, 1980), ch. I, pt. 1, 25–29.
3. G. W. F. Hegel, *Philosophie de l'esprit*, vol. 3 in *Encyclopédie des Sciences Philosophiques* trans. Bernard Bourgeois (Paris: Vrin, 1988), addition # 405, pt. 1, 468.
4. Kierkegaard, *The Concept of Anxiety*, ch. 1, pt. 6, 49.

Chapter 15. Dream, Imagination, Reality

1. Jean Laplanche, *Problématique V. Le Baquet: Transcendance du transfert* (Paris: Presses Universitaires de France, 1987).
2. Serge Viderman, *La Construction de l'espace analytique* (Paris: Denoël, 1970).
3. Sigmund Freud, "Project for a Scientific Psychology" in *The Origins of Psycho-Analysis: Letters to Wilhelm Fliess, Drafts and Notes, 1887–1902*, trans. Eric Mosbacher and James Strachey (New York: Basic Books, 1954), 347–445.
4. Michel de Montaigne, Essais III: 3; in *The Complete Works of Montaigne*, trans. Donald M. Frame (Stanford: Stanford University Press 1948/1957), 637.
5. Giacomo Casanova, *History of My Life*, trans. Willard R. Trask (New York: Harcourt, Brace and World, 1966), 46.

Acknowledgments

"Nobody" was previously published in French in *Études freudi-ennes* (May 1982). An earlier translation has appeared under the title "Nobody—Anybody—Somebody" in *Psychoanalytic Inquiry* 4:2 (1984), 163–70.

"Uncertainty" previously appeared in French in *Passé-Présent* (1982).

"The Effectiveness of Psychoanalysis" previously appeared in *Modern Language Notes* 97:4 (1982), 775–86.

"On the Epistemology of Psychoanalysis" was previously published in French in *Le moi et l'autre* (Paris: Denoël, 1985). A previous translation appeared in *Modern Language Notes* 99:4 (1984), 928–40.

"The Laboratory of Cruelty" is based on a lecture given during the workshops of the ANREP, Association nationale pour la recherche de l'étude en psychologie (National Association for Scholarly Research in Psychology) in November 1985. It appeared in the *Cahiers de l'ANREP* nos. 3–4 (1986), 17–22.

"The Components of Freud's Style" was originally a lecture given in Besançon during a philosophy conference held in December 1986. It was previously published under the title "Analytique, rhétorique, poétique" in *Nervure, Journal de psychiatrie* (February 1990), 47–51.

"On Transference Neurosis" was originally presented to a group of psychiatrists in Paris on May 31, 1987.

"Pedagogue or Mystagogue" was originally presented at a colloquium on psychoanalysis and pedagogy that was held by the Freudian Circle in Geneva, on November 7, 1987.

"Transmitting Anxiety," originally presented at the Collège des

Psychanalystes in June 1987, was previously published in French in *Psychanalystes*, 25 (October 1987), 23–30.

Part of "On the End of Analysis and Self-Hypnosis as a Cure" appeared in French in *Études freudiennes* 30 (October, 1987), 39–48.

"In Certain Cases" was originally presented to the medical staff of the Maison Blanche Hospital in October 1986. It previously appeared in French in *Etudes freudiennes* 30 (October 1987), 131–40.

"The Cure" appeared in French in *Le Bloc-Notes de la psychanalyse* (October 1988), 123–34.

"A Condition of Liberty" appeared in French in *Psychanalystes, 30* (January 1989), 49–56.

"What Does It Mean to Be a Psychoanalyst?" was initially a lecture given in São Paolo in April 1991 during a meeting of four Brazilian psychoanalytic associations. It was published in French in *Esquisses psychanalytiques* (Spring 1992), 161–67.

"Dream, Imagination, Reality" was originally delivered during a symposium in Lyon in November, 1992, at the Charles-Baudoin International Institute of Psychoanalysis. It appeared in French in *Action et Pensée* (April 1993), 33–48.

Index